St. Louis Community College

Jake O'Shaughnessey's SOURDOUGH BOOK

JAKE O'SHAUGHNESSEY'S

Sourdough Book

by Timothy Firnstahl

Illustrations by Susan Hughes

SAN FRANCISCO BOOK COMPANY, INC.

San Francisco 1976

Printed in the United States of America

Library of Congress Cataloging in Publication Data

Firnstahl, Timothy, 1943-
    Jake O'Shaughnessey's sourdough book.

    Includes index.
    1.   Bread.   2.   Pancakes, Waffles, etc.
3.   Baking.   I.   Title.   II.   Title: Sourdough
book.
TX769.F52   641.6'3'11   76-9766
ISBN 0-913374-30-X (cloth)
ISBN 0-913374-31-8 (paperback)

Simon and Schuster Order Number 22285 (cloth); 22286 (paper)

Trade distribution by Simon and Schuster
A Gulf + Western Company

10 9 8 7 6 5 4 3 2 1

This book is lovingly dedicated

to my wife MERRIANN

CONTENTS

The Story of JAKE O'SHAUGHNESSEY'S

A convivial roustabout by the name of Jake O'Shaughnessey opened a soon-to-be-famous saloon in Seattle in August of 1897. It was Jake's intent to provide first-quality libations and fine Northwest fare to the thousands of Yankee shopkeepers, farmers, trollops, drummers, and doctors who flooded Seattle on their way to the Far North and gold. All who knew Jake found he operated his establishment boisterously and greatly relished his own good food and drink and an occasional fisticuff.

In 1974, after an absence of nearly seventy-five years, Jake O'Shaughnessey's was re-established in Seattle. It is of course dedicated to the memory of Mr. O'Shaughnessey and the same

ix

fine food and drink he shared with his friends and guests.

This book is the outcome of research into the sourdough breads and other victuals that were featured in the original saloon. Its purpose is to acquaint good cooks and bakers everywhere with the art of sourdough cookery as it has been practiced through the generations with uniquely delicious results.

FOREWORD

The art of sourdough requires more effort and time than does most other cooking. This might make some wonder as to why it's worth the bother; after all, we're not in the same position as was the Gold Rush prospector. He had the choice of maintaining his own wild yeast culture and having fresh bread and biscuits as a result, or eating weevily, hard-as-a-rock sea biscuit. It's not too difficult to see why he kept his sourdough pot in good repair.

There are many good reasons for using sourdough, but the first that comes to my mind is flavor. Sourdough provides its user with incomparably fine baked goods. Nothing can match its zest and tang because the long, slow aging process which sourdough requires gives it a savor which has no equal. It's butter instead of margarine. It's a bottle of mature Cabernet Sauvignon instead of something that comes from a gallon jug with a twist cap. It's freshly squeezed orange juice instead of frozen. In short, it's honest and genuine instead of a mimicry of the real thing.

The worth of sourdough, however, cannot be measured solely in terms of gustatory delight. In addition to its superb flavor, there are other appealing aspects to be found in the art of sourdough cookery. Wild yeast has an individuality all its own. For being a wholly unique and interesting way of cooking, sourdough surely stands in the forefront. You are afforded the opportunity of making something in your own home that simply cannot be purchased at a super-market. The freezer cases, shelves, and bakery counters of these flashy, plastic-chrome arcades have never had in them the likes of such flavorful and nourishing goods as bannock, johnny-cake, and billycan bread. And your local baker has probably never heard of such delectable desserts and breads as green apple duff, cherry pandowdy and sourcream herb bread, let alone offered them for sale. If lately you've been suppressing a desire for something new and different, here's your chance. Sourdough is an edible adventure away from the mundane.

The baked goods you will make using sourdough are not only succulent and discrete, but they are also free from the texturizers, artificial flavorings and preservatives so prevalent in today's commercial baking. While this cookbook was not written specifically with natural foods in mind, you can draw upon the satisfaction of knowing the things you prepare with sourdough are the same kind of wholesome foods your great-great-grandmother made with loving care over a century ago.

In those no-nonsense days before the plague of television, a good, robust meal meant a great deal. Exceptional recipes were carefully guarded and handed down from generation to generation as though they were holy writ. This book contains a thesaurus of sourdough recipes which will bring you the same hearty pleasure enjoyed by those who lived before the turn of the century. These highly esteemed old sourdough recipes were garnered from divers sources. Some were found in old letters, others were procured from friends, and the rare book sections of various libraries proved to be abundant springs of information. Most of these recipes have interesting histories, and where probity allows, their colorful stories have been included.

While some adjustments were necessary in the interest of modern convenience, every effort has been made to keep recipes in their original form. In using this book, you will partake of the same sourdough fare that was relished by our forefathers. The art of sourdough cookery will take you back to a time when food was really food and had flavor to boot!

Sourdough will also give you a deep sense of personal satisfaction. Not only are you favored with the opportunity of making something far better than that which can be purchased, but also sourdough cookery provides quite a challenge. You will find that the nurturing of wild yeast is not the same as using a mix to make a cake. The sourdough pot demands perseverance, understanding, and a degree of fiddling to master it. Developing your sourdough skill will require effort, but when that first crusty, fragrant loaf comes from the oven, no one will need to tell you that the time spent was worthwhile indeed.

Seattle, Washington
January 1976

TIM FIRNSTAHL

THE FACT AND FANCY OF SOURDOUGH

Aside from fire, the utilization of wild yeast is man's oldest method of processing food. In their first use of what was to become the sourdough pot, our early ancestors probably were more interested in a jug of heady, freshly fermented beer than leavened bread. The Mesopotamians were successfully brewing beer six thousand years before the birth of Christ, but it wasn't until three thousand years later that the Egyptians finally figured out how to use wild yeast to raise their bread. From that point bread became a mainstay of the Egyptian diet and infused all of Western civilization. Bread was so prized that it was put in the tombs of the pharaohs and oftentimes was used as a form of pay. Hieroglyphics relate that freemen building certain of the pyramids were given two crocks of beer and four loaves of bread for a day's labor.

In ancient Greece and Rome baking became a highly accomplished art with hundreds of bread varieties being developed. Baking flourished and guilds were formed which were to last until modern times.

During the Middle Ages bread was not only eaten but also was used as tableware. Plates, eating utensils, and the like that were common during the period of the Roman Empire disappeared with its downfall. A slice of wild yeast bread known as a trencher was used as a plate and the crust from it sufficed as a spoon. At the end of the meal the trenchers were usually collected for distribution to the poor.

Although the Indians of America did not use wild yeast, the sourdough pot couldn't have arrived in the New World much sooner than it did. Columbus was a great lover of bread and always took a crock of yeast with him whenever he sailed. History tells us that at least one of the three Spanish ships which first landed in this hemisphere was equipped with a sourdough pot. Of course, all the settlers to the American colonies brought crocks of wild yeast with them for their bread and beer making. Breweries and flour mills were among the first businesses in America.

As our country grew, most homes maintained a sourdough pot. From these came the toothsome breadstuffs that America grew up on. Wagons moving Westward had sourdough aboard, and fresh bread at the end of a long day's difficult travel was a much-welcomed reward.

The word *sourdough* was first made legend with the California Gold Rush of 1849. The forty-niners always seemed to have a container of sourdough with them, providing otherwise unobtainable baked goods. The word *sourdough* became so associated with the gold seekers that eventually the words *sourdough* and *prospector* came to mean the same thing.

After the California Gold Rush the knowledge of sourdough spread to Alaska where the lore became a part of the land. It was there that the legend of sourdough fully developed. Although the Yukon Gold Rush occurred in 1897, gold had been successfully panned there for many years prior to that time. The men who hunted for gold before the great influx were the true pioneers of the North. They were a rugged and independent breed, living off the land and by their wits.

Hardship and loneliness were an accepted part of life. The gold digger would go sometimes for months at a time without seeing another white man. Life was difficult, but the hope of gold and the freedom of Alaska and the Yukon were far better than the trample of civilization to the south.

The fare of these men was simple. They hunted for their meat: bear, moose, caribou, and other wild game; and their sourdough pot provided them with fresh, delicious bread, biscuits, and griddlecakes. Beans were used a good deal, as was rice. With each meal, tea was invariably taken as the beverage. Since all drinking water was boiled from snow, it was quick to fix. Coffee became prevalent only after the Rush of '97. In the early days milk was impossible to get, and eggs sold for as much as five dollars a dozen. The sourdoughs' diet was usually more than adequate but occasionally scurvy would set in, a condition which was treated with tea made from spruce boughs. It must have worked because many an old-timer lived well into his eighties.

7

The fresh meat he hunted and the sourdough pot provided the mainstay of the prospector's diet. He used his wild yeast with efficiency and creativity. Bread could always be made in a gold dust pan, put near the fire to rise, and then moved closer to bake. Biscuits were popular because they could be made without much bother. A great favorite was billycan biscuits. A billycan was a stout container with a lid. It was used primarily as a small larder for fresh meat, but it had many other uses also. For biscuit making it worked especially well. All that had to be done at the end of a long day was to throw some sourdough into the can along with flour, water, bear grease, sugar, a pinch of salt, and maybe some saleratus (baking soda), if it was available. (Bear fat was prized in biscuits because of its good mild flavor.) The lid would be put on the can after mixing the dough. The can would then be set aside so the dough could puff up and then be baked later . . . all in the same container.

Sourdough was such an important part of the sourdough's diet that wherever he went, the starter always went along, carefully packed in the sourdough's bindle where the cold could not penetrate the thick blankets of his bedroll. At night, without fail, he would protect his starter from the raw, arctic nights by keeping it in his bedroll and sleeping with it. It was believed that any time mercury froze (−40°F), it certainly wouldn't help a starter, and the mercury froze almost every night during the long cold winters. The loss of a starter in midwinter was by a sourdough's standards a catastrophe. Unless he could get another one from a friend, it usually meant having to go without breadstuffs for three or four months. During the cold of winter it was impossible to coax a wild yeast out of the air and have it grow. A starter was looked after as closely as a poke of gold.

Siwashing (meaning, in the vernacular of the era, "to camp out," "to make camp," etc.) tested the ingenuity of the prospector and the versatility of his starter. While on the trail the prospector was without the benefit of his fireplace which provided him with even, steady heat. He had to make do with a windblown campfire. But never at a loss, he used a technique for making his bread which he called stick-baking. With a stream always nearby he would find a willow tree, cut off a small branch, and trim off the bark. Using bacon, he'd grease the end of the skewer and then wrap dough around it. By pushing the stick in the ground near the fire he would only have to turn it occasionally to have hot, freshly baked bread with his beans and salt pork . . . a real delicacy considering his being in the middle of the wilderness.

There was another way a sourdough baked bread while traveling. When so inclined, he might decide to do some "dirt bakin'." This required a little more effort, but the result was well worth the labor because it gave him a bread supply for several days. In the early part of the evening the dough would be prepared and allowed to rise in a Dutch oven near the fire. After the bread had pretty well risen, the sourdough would gently move his fire a foot or two to one side, exposing the ground underneath. By this time the fire would have thawed the earth sufficiently so a shallow pit could be scooped out. Coals from the fire were put into the pit, and a little fresh wood was added. Once the fire in the pit had burned to embers, the Dutch oven was put in and more embers were added to the sides and top, thus baking the bread. As you can imagine, dirt bakin' took some practice, but an old-timer knew his fires, and in the morning he would enjoy fresh bread which often was still warm.

The sourdough crock was loved not only for the excellent bread and savory flapjacks made from it, but also because the venerable pot had a myriad of other unlikely uses. A good starter served as a veritable cornucopia, as versatile as its owner. Our hinterland heroes lived hun-

9

dreds of miles from civilization and all they possessed had to be used to its maximum potential. In the hands of a sourdough, a humble container of wild yeast was used for purposes which today stretch our imagination.

Possibly a starter's most improbable usage was as medicine. Often, not having a doctor within five hundred miles left the sourdough completely to his own devices. He found it necessary to minister to his needs with what he had, and as a healing poultice, starter had no peer. A scoop of the gooey white paste, heated on the stove and then applied liberally to the affected area, worked surprisingly well. This method was used on every external ailment imaginable. The 1898 edition of the *International Cyclopedia* ("A Compendium of Human Knowledge") comments on the effectiveness of *Cataplasma fermenti* (yeast poultice) as being "a stimulant and antiseptic in cases of indolent ulcers and other maladies." There was little a starter wasn't used to remedy: cuts, burns, sores, bruises, wounds, aches, and pains. All received the same treatment. As a last resort an old prospector might even use his wild yeast for stomach distress. A teaspoon of raw starter taken internally was good for what ailed him. Raw starter is vile stuff, especially the way the old prospectors used to keep it, so they must have thought that if it didn't kill them it would surely work a cure.

Rifles carried by the early Gold Rushers often had brass fittings of one sort or another. A little starter applied to these and allowed to sit a minute or two did a fine job of polishing. Belt buckles or anything else made of brass or copper could be made to look like new again when rubbed with sourdough.

Another backwoods use of sourdough was as an adhesive. As glue, starter came close to being liquid iron, and for the prospector it worked far better than anything he could buy. He used it to glue paper, cloth, wood, leather and anything else that was porous, including crockery, provided that it wasn't submerged in water too often. Even log cabins were chinked with starter, but the stories we hear about using sourdough to resole boots probably fall into the same category as the claim that a sourdough hotcake makes a helluva roof shingle.

Aside from its applications in baking, sourdough was used most often to provide a form of libation. Given warmth and sufficient time, a clear nefarious liquid rises to the top of all starters. A machination of the devil, prospectors called it hooch. It was strong enough to corn even the most hearty of individuals. With an alcoholic content of 15 per cent, a smell kinder to kerosene, and the taste of high grade mineral spirits, it wasn't much competition for the "store boughten red eye." But to a forlorn prospector snowed in his cabin in the middle of an Alaskan winter, it was ambrosia in its sublimest form. Again in a display of wilderness creativity, a sourdough might refine his hooch with a crude still made from the barrel of an old 45-90 rifle. This would give him a kind of "white mule" that could send him on an unforgettable shindy. Many a prospector passed away the confinement in his cabin with his sourdough pot bubbling enough hooch to keep him blissfully sotted the whole time. As the snow melted, he would eventually emerge with a horrendous case of the jim-jams and a solemn vow never to imbibe the stuff again. Such an affirmation was usually good for at least three days.

Before leaving the era of the Alaskan sourdough, we would be remiss not to mention two of his most outstanding culinary achievements. The first of these immortal viands is the inimitable beanhole bean. For those unfortunates who have not been graced with knowledge of this most savory food, let us delve further.

As with dirt bakin', the prospector would fill the bottom of a hole with hot coals. Using a stout billycan filled with his favorite beanhole bean recipe, he would put this into the pit and shovel more burning embers over the can, being careful to cover it completely. A day or two later when he was sure that all had been simmered to mouth-watering tenderness, he would unearth his cache and relish his creation.

Not only was the beanhole bean a flavorful repast, but it had excellent keeping qualities. Henry Davis, an old-timer of that period, reported that these beans could be cooked ahead and then left outside to freeze. Whenever he wanted beans, he just went out and broke off a chunk. According to Davis, it didn't take long to "rustle up a real good grub pile."

So that you might enjoy the delight to be found in beanhole beans, I have included a recipe. I feel, however, the need to warn you not to be put off by its simplicity. Granted the ingredients are prosaic, but the long slow cooking produced a marriage of flavors far surpassing anything that might be expected as an ultimate outcome. Beanhole beans are wholly unlike Boston baked beans, chili, or some watery-sauced pork and beans from a can. By all means afford yourself the opportunity of enjoying this superb favorite of the sourdoughs.

Old-Timer's Beanhole Beans

Note: The molasses, chili peppers and salt can be adjusted to suit individual tastes.

1½ qts. water (6 cups)
¼ lb. salt pork, diced
2 medium onions,
   coarsely chopped
½ cup molasses

2 cups washed and sorted
   pinto beans
1 red chili pepper, whole
1 teaspoon salt
2 cloves of garlic, minced

Soak the beans overnight. Start the preparation of the beans early the next day because this dish requires 9 to 10 hours of moderate slow cooking.

Start

Put beans, water, salt, and chili pepper into a heavy pot. Start the cooking process on very low heat. Do not allow the mixture to boil. Keep covered.

5th Hour

Sauté the salt pork until it is rendered quite crisp. Then add the onion and garlic and continue to sauté until the onion is brown. Stir the mixture into the beans. Do this with care because the beans will be soft and break easily. Add the molasses. Leave the pot uncovered so the liquid can start to reduce. Do not increase the cooking temperature;

maintain the low heat. The long cooking process is what develops the true Beanhole Bean flavor.

9th to 11th Hours

The beans should be very tender and the bean pot liquor should be reduced to a rich sauce. When dishing, be careful not to crush the beans because they will be very tender. Enjoy! Depending on how hungry your trenchermen are, this recipe serves from two to four.

The second of our comestibles is stew. Although this was not an invention of the Alaskan Gold Rusher, we have included it here because the sourdough was an ardent user of the Dutch oven. From his dinner pot came such savory spoon meat as to preclude the need for all else save sourdough biscuits or bread. Since the original recipe called for such as caribou or moose meat, murphies (potatoes), and sloshes of water as needed, license has been taken to update the instructions for today's home use.

Shank Burgoo with Dumplings

14

Stew:

3 lbs. of beef shank bones with plenty of meat still on them.
1 large onion, sliced   2 potatoes, peeled and quartered

2 carrots, peeled and whole
1 turnip, peeled and quartered

1 medium can of tomatoes
Seasonings to taste

Dumplings:

1 egg, beaten
Bone marrow from the shanks

½ teaspoon salt
Flour, as needed

You will have to find a real live butcher if you want to prepare this dish. Have the butcher cut the shank bones into 3-inch pieces. Also have him split the bones so you can remove the marrow. Scrape the marrow from the bones and cover the shanks with salted water, boiling them for 1 hour. Add the vegetables and cook until they start to become tender. To make the dumplings, add the egg to warm marrow and salt. Mash. Add sufficient flour to this mixture so that dumplings can be rolled using the palms of your hands. The dumplings should be about the size of a small walnut. Drop them into the boiling stew, cover, and simmer for about 45 minutes. Serves about four.

Over the past sixty years the use of sourdough has dwindled to almost nothing. Even folks in their eighties will attest to the fact that when they were young they used packaged yeast in their bread making. The decline of sourdough usage has been especially unfortunate because some of the most tasty victuals ever to cross a palate are made with it. As of late, however, sourdough has been enjoying a much welcomed resurgence. People are becoming interested in the amazing qualities of wild yeast and are again beginning to engage in the entertaining and absorbing art of sourdough cookery. Regrettably, accurate information about sourdough is difficult to obtain. There are many reasons for this, the foremost being that the art has almost disappeared. Even professional bakers almost never produce sourdough. The few bakers who still work exclusively with sourdough are located primarily in the San Francisco Bay area, where the most famous of all sourdough bread is baked. These highly skilled men tend to be taciturn about their profession. Those who will give you a little of their time claim that their beautiful bread is the result of anything from the water they use to the San Francisco fog. All this hokum adds to the fun and lore of sourdough but does not do much to help the *aficionado* who wants to make sourdough bread and other delicacies in his home.

In an attempt to gain knowledge about sourdough one might think of turning to his local baker. Although he no doubt makes excellent cakes and ordinary yeast breads, his grasp of sourdough is probably limited. Most likely he has never been trained in the use and nurturing of sourdough and has consequently never baked with it. He is probably as much misled by the fiction that surrounds the subject as the rest of us. Ordinarily, when he makes what he calls sourdough bread, it comes from one of the many pre-made, commercial mixes which are available to him. These produce only a fair imitation of the real thing.

Cookbooks for the most part are also of little assistance. About one cookbook in twenty-five even makes mention of sourdough. This dearth of written information is the result of public acceptance of commercial yeast and baking powder. Since the turn of the century these products have received wide distribution, and cookbook authors have been inclined to delete sourdough cookery from their works as being obsolete and old-fashioned. Those current cookbooks which do discuss sourdough most likely contain misinformation and often reflect the fact that sourdough baking has almost become a lost art. For example, they invariably call for substantial amounts of commercial yeast in their "sourdough" recipes. Such instructions do not take into consideration that the flavor of sourdough is greatly diminished with the addition of yeast to sourdough bread. Also recommended in bread recipes is the use of baking soda, which abrogates the flavor of sourdough and thus ruins what might have turned out to be exceptional bread. Excessive amounts of baking soda are frequently called for in sourdough flapjacks and biscuits. So much soda is normally specified that the sourdough devotee can scarcely distinguish between his sourdough griddlecakes or biscuits and the ordinary variety. This is especially frustrating when it is considered that in all likelihood our hapless sourdough cook patiently aged his sourdough for twelve to twenty-four hours to develop a hearty robust flavor, only to have it ruined by the addition of too much bicarbonate of soda.

Probably the worst of all offenses perpetuated by these supposed modern-day gastronomical guides is the mixing of milk with starter. Nothing will ruin a good pot of wild yeast faster than using milk instead of plain water. Milk inhibits the growth of yeast and should never be used when replenishing a starter. Flour and water are the only things that should ever find their way into your sourdough starter because all else will defile your carefully safeguarded vessel.

Cookbooks which appear to be written especially for women sometimes verge on being prissy when it comes to our subject. Proper care of sourdough is important, but being finicky about the wrong things can do more harm than good. Some of these cookbooks go so far as to suggest that sourdough starter be thrown away when it begins to look and smell a mite wicked. Such a sacrilege is enough to make any Gold Rush prospector turn in his grave. Sourdough pots naturally tend to be on the feral side and the idea of discarding a sourdough pot because it smells or looks bad is contradictory to good sourdough cookery. Don't let our somewhat exaggerated twentieth century sense of what is sanitary deceive you. As a pot of sourdough is kept through the years, its flavor matures and improves with each usage. And any sourdough pot can be put into an acceptable state for even the most scrupulous of individuals. Later it will be explained how prospectors used a technique they called "sweetening the pot" to make their overly potent sourdough tolerable again. This procedure can bring even the most seemingly unwholesome and lifeless sourdough back to vigor. There is rarely, if ever, a need to throw out a sourdough pot.

The women's cookbooks therefore aren't much help, but neither are those written mainly for men. The so-called wilderness cookbooks almost always have something to say about sourdough and by the same token are usually a trove of misinformation. They seem to be plagued by misconstruing the lore of days past. Some still maintain that sourdough should never be allowed to freeze. This is probably a holdover from the Gold Rush prospector's mistaken belief that he had to sleep with his sourdough pot while on the trail for fear of the cold killing his precious provender. Actually, sourdough freezes very well and can be kept frozen almost indefinitely. Another holdover found in these books is that bread dough should not be kneaded. By far the lightest and tastiest breads are those which are thoroughly kneaded. Old time camp cooks and prospectors believed that kneading knocked out the gases which raised bread. It was thought that for the best results throwing the bread together beat coddling it along. That may seem to be a credible theory, but in truth one of the keys to good sourdough bread making is long, careful kneading.

All the confusing lore about sourdough is best approached with a bit of twinkle in your eye. While the old wives' tales are interesting, don't let the stories dismay you. Sourdough cookery is *easy*. Once you come to understand how sourdough works, you will execute the recipes in this book with ease and will probably create a few of your own.

There are, however, some essential factors to bear in mind. The first is time. Sourdough is an anomaly in today's fast-paced society. It takes much longer to work than the "modern" methods you're probably used to. While cake mixes and frozen biscuits require just a few minutes and a recipe for bread using commercial yeast needs but several hours, sourdough cookery is oftentimes measured in days. The extended period of time sourdough baking requires produces a fine flavor that can only be accomplished with your patience and wild yeast's easy-going pace. You will not be able to hurry things along because sourdough will not be rushed. Don't be disheartened, because you'll soon find yourself planning on Wednesday to bake unbelievably good bread on Friday. Once you get a feel for sourdough's timetable, the length of time it entails will not pose any kind of problem.

Always remember that when you are working with sourdough it is a living, growing thing. It requires feeding and care just like all things which are alive. Some folks develop a real affection for their pots and frequently give them nicknames. Once you come to understand the nature of your wild yeast and the range of things it can do, you may do the same.

THE STARTER

The heart of all sourdough baking is the starter. It is a simple combination of flour and water which contains a large number of live, wild yeast cells. Starter derives its name from the fact that a small amount of this mixture is taken from its container and used to "start" the fermentation of a hotcake batter or some other sourdough food. Starter is the "start" of all sourdough cooking and puts the wild yeast into a sourdough recipe. This establishes the fermentation process which provides the leavening gas and that admirable flavor so much enjoyed by all.

When a portion of starter is used, an equal amount of flour and water is always returned to the starter container. Thus a starter is constantly maintained in the same amount. It's perpetual and, if cared for properly, will last indefinitely. A crock of starter is your own permanent wild yeast factory.

Wild yeast is everywhere. Through the ages man has never had much difficulty in securing it because it has the penchant for floating in the air. It merely has to land where there is moisture and food and it will begin to grow and multiply. This might lead some to believe mistakenly that all one need do is mix up some flour with water and in no time there will be a bucket of starter fit for use by the most discerning gourmand. Unfortunately, it's not quite that simple.

There are thousands of wild yeasts that can be caught from the air. Yeast hunting is a little like fishing; it requires the helping hand of Providence because the quality of wild yeasts vary tremendously. Some are fair, others poor, and there are those few specimens that are truly exceptional. This is why the loss of a good sourdough pot to an Alaskan gold digger was a serious problem. If need be, he'd brave the elements and walk miles to get another bit of starter from a friend who had a worthy pot. Trying to catch a good replacement was just too difficult.

Starting A Starter

Before starting a starter, you will want to select the right container for it. Starters are pretty particular about where they live. Glass, wood, crockery, or polyethylene containers of 1-quart capacity all work well. If you aren't a staunch traditionalist, plastic containers are best because they're light, easy to clean, and unbreakable. Choose a container with a lid so that your starter is protected and contaminants are kept out. The lid should not be airtight, though, because wild yeast needs air to live.

When choosing your sourdough container, make sure that it is not one of metal. No metal containers of any kind are suitable for use with a starter. Wild yeast produces rather potent acids which can corrode metal, and this corrosion can mix with the starter, thus killing it.

It is a good idea once the container has been selected to label it. Unwitting members of your household, uninitiated to the ways of sourdough, might think they are doing you a favor by throwing away a vessel of starter as being something that has "spoiled." Save the embarrassment of having to tell them the container of evil-smelling fluid they so helpfully disposed of for you was the progenitor of the flapjacks and breads about which they raved.

There are two methods for starting a starter. The first is easier and guaranteed to work while the second is harder, more interesting, and will invariably produce a better starter. You make the choice.

METHOD I

Thoroughly wash the container you have selected for your starter. This will prevent contamination by unwanted organisms. Mix a ¼-ounce packet of dry yeast (Fleischmann, Red Star, etc.) with 2 cups of flour and 1½ cups of warm water. Stir and set the preparation aside in a warm place for three days. At the end of this period your starter will be bubbly and will smell of yeast mixed with a touch of alcohol. This aroma is natural and lets you know the domesticated yeast that you started with has again turned wild and is ready for use. You will then have 2 cups of starter to put to task.

As this new starter is used, it will materially improve in its flavor-giving qualities. You will find that after about two weeks use it will start to come into its own and continue to get better.

23

Many different kinds of sourdough starter can be made by using various types of yeast. Your local store for wine making has a marvelous collection of various yeasts that can be made into a starter. Or get a bit of starter from a friend. Each will be a wee different; just follow the basic instructions given above.

METHOD II

If you're the adventuresome type, you might want to try some wild yeast hunting of your own. There are hundreds of varieties of this flora that can be caught, and you might be able to hook one of the excellent types. There is no guarantee that you will catch one of any kind, but here's what to do if you want to try your luck.

Go to a health foods store and buy a quart of raw (unpasteurized) whole milk. Use all but 1½ cups of it. Pour this into a bowl, cover with cheesecloth and set aside for 3 to 4 days. Once the milk has soured very thoroughly, mix 2 cups of flour into it, recover and let work another 24 hours before using.

Depending upon the beneficence of Mother Nature, you may not have caught any wild yeast at all. In that case, no bubbling will be present in the mixture and it's time to try again. If bubbles are present, you will have caught a wild yeast ranging from good to exceptional. Using it for a while will let you know into which category it falls. If you have caught a good one, happily it will improve the longer you keep and use it.

Replenishing a Starter

Once starter is up and going it should be kept in the refrigerator between uses. This will keep the wild yeast from growing too much (over-fermenting) and partially dying as a result. Over-fermented starter does not work well. Refrigeration helps to eliminate this problem by slowing the yeast growth to a point where, although the starter is not used daily, there will be sufficient food and moisture for the yeast to feed on and remain healthy.

Each time a starter is used, what is taken out must be put back in the form of all-purpose flour and water. This provides the wild yeast in the starter with new nourishment and also insures that a starter is perpetuated so that you never run out of it. Putting flour and water into a sourdough pot after a like amount of starter has been taken out is called replenishing. If your starter is lumpy after it has been replenished, the wild yeast will make it smooth again as the mixture ripens.

A newly replenished starter is also very active. If left in a warm place, it will double in bulk and this is why a starter container of 1-quart capacity is recommended.

All the recipes in this book call for the use of either 1 cup or 1 tablespoon of starter. It is a good idea when removing any of these two amounts to stir the starter so that the gas bubbles are knocked out. This results in a more accurate measure.

The removal of 1 cup of starter is replenished by adding 1 cup of white flour and ¾ cup of water. This might seem as though it's too much, but when the two are mixed they equal about a cup. To replenish the removal of 1 tablespoon of starter, discard all the remaining starter but 1 tablespoon. Mix this tablespoon with 2 cups of flour and 1½ cups of warm water. Always remember, the Golden Rule of sourdough cookery: The amount of starter taken or discarded must be replaced with a like amount of flour and water. Nevertheless, even the most proficient sourdough cooks forget the replenishing rule at one time or another. Should this happen to you, don't panic. A small amount of starter can go a long, long way. For example, if you have just 1 cup of starter left instead of the normal 2 cups, go ahead and begin a recipe using the last cup, but leave a tablespoon or so in the container. To this add 2 cups of flour and 1½ cups of warm water and stir. Set the container aside in a warm place for a day or two, and your starter will come back to full potency, ready again for use.

Sweetening the Pot

Most likely you will not use your starter on a daily basis. Despite refrigeration, a starter continues to grow and after just a day or two, begins to over-age. A starter which has been allowed to mature too long is characterized by a lack of bubbling, a layer of hooch floating on its surface and sometimes an odor which makes even the most eager of sourdoughphiles wince. Whatever you do, don't throw your starter away. A starter in this condition can easily be revitalized. The prospectors called the procedure of bringing an old starter back to life "sweetening the pot." Using this technique can render even the most tempestuous looking and smelling of pots docile once more. Refrigerated starters which have been left unattended and unused for months at a time and have turned to cauldrons containing the most pernicious of unsightly goos can be made fresh and acceptable again. Don't let the sinister appearance of an old starter fool you.

Sweetening the pot is simple. Discard all but 1 tablespoon of the starter, putting this amount aside in a separate container. If the starter is particularly old, reserve a portion that is free from mold or anything else that looks suspect. Wash the sourdough container and return the tablespoon of old starter to it. Put 2 cups of flour and 1½ cups of warm water into the pot and mix. Allow the newly sweetened pot to sit for 24 hours in a warm place before using it. At the end of this period, your starter will be as good as new. However, when a starter has not been used for a month or more, it is a good idea to go through the complete cycle of sweetening the pot two or three times before using it. In those instances where a refrigerated starter has not been used for three months or more, a pot may have to be sweetened as many as five or six times before it comes back to vigor. The first time or two simply won't bring the dormant wild yeast to life. Just remember that each time a pot is sweetened, the process requires the *complete* cycle: discarding all but 1 tablespoon of starter, replenishing with 2 cups of flour and 1½ cups warm water, and developing for 24 hours at 72° to 80°. This procedure will insure a starter that is in perfect condition.

27

When a pot is replenished or sweetened, you are in effect, feeding the wild yeast. What goes into a container of sourdough is very important. To guarantee that your starter stays in good shape, use only flour and water. All other things such as milk, salt, eggs, and so on tend to slow the rate of wild yeast growth and promote molding. Great injury can be done to a starter when the wrong things are added to it. People are sometimes tempted to put hotcake batter or other raw sourdough left-overs into their pots to stretch them, but these will only pollute the mixture. Remember always to use only flour and warm water.

General Starter Care

Temperature has a marked effect on starter. Refrigeration *slows* the rate of wild yeast growth, but freezing will successfully stop its growth altogether with no ill effect. A starter can be held for months at a time in this fashion, and it's a good way to keep it if you're not planning to use it for a while. After a starter has been frozen, it's best to let it thaw completely and then sweeten it once as described above before using. This allows the yeast a chance to bounce back.

Although low temperatures do not injure a starter, extremely high temperatures can be ruinous. Wild yeast thrives at a temperature of 75° or slightly higher, but at 110° and above it begins to react adversely. Whenever water is added to a starter it should be warm but not hot. At 120° the flour in a starter begins to cook and this obviously isn't beneficial to the well-being of a wild yeast. It's a good idea to keep a starter away from burners, hot ovens, and other sources of high heat that can do harm to your valuable repository. If for some reason you want to speed up the action of the wild yeast, find a draft free spot that has a temperature between 75° and 110°.

Occasionally you will want to clean your starter container. In the old days a prospector would swallow his teeth at such a suggestion because during those times it was thought the worse a starter looked, the better it worked. Unfortunately, some worked only about as well as they looked for lack of proper care. Your starter will work much better if it's not allowed to degenerate to the state many were allowed to reach during the Gold Rush era.

The temperature of the water you use for cleaning a starter container has a great deal to do with how easily it's cleaned. First, pour the starter into a non-metallic bowl and cover. Start washing the container, using a brush, warm water, and dishwashing soap. Make certain that you use warm water because hot water turns starter to a sticky, clinging mass which will make your task fit only for a scullion. Warm water does the best job. If the container is especially crusty, let it soak for several hours before attempting to wash it.

Should you ever spill starter, take pains to wipe it up immediately. When the stuff dries, it's remarkably similar to cement. You will need something akin to a cold chisel and hammer to get it off once it's hardened. Don't find out why the prospectors had good reason for using it as a glue.

SUNDRY SOURDOUGH SUSTENANCE

This section will provide you with a good introduction to the nearly lost art of sourdough cuisine. You will find an interesting assortment of recipes for flapjacks, biscuits, quickbreads, and desserts. These are not as difficult as the bread recipes later in the book, and so they make an ideal starting point for your first experiences with wild yeast. You can practice and gain a feel for the handling of sourdough before going on to the more involved bread-making procedures.

Ambrosia Batter

Almost all the recipes found in Sundry Sourdough Sustenance begin with a mixture of starter, flour and water which is allowed to ripen for twenty-four hours between 75° and 80° before being used. The name of this concoction is taken from the food of the gods often referred to in Greek mythology. The title is appropriate considering the various delectable things that can be made with it. No doubt when you mix up your first batch of sourdough griddlecakes or biscuits, you'll agree. Here's how to make it:

1 cup starter
1 cup water   1½ cups white all-purpose flour

Mix the above ingredients in a 2-quart bowl, cover and set aside for 24 hours in a place where the temperature ranges between 75° and 80°. Remember to use only a bowl made of glass or crockery, not metal. Also make sure that your bowl is large enough to allow the mixture to double in volume without spilling over the side. Ambrosia Batter is burdensome to clean up, especially after it has dried.

Replenish the starter with 1 cup of flour and ¾ cup of warm water.

A few recipes call for a half recipe of Ambrosia Batter. This is made using ½ cup of starter, ½ cup of water and ¾ cup of white all-purpose flour. The starter pot should be replenished with just under ½ cup of flour and ¼ cup of warm water. The rest of the procedures are identical to those given above.

When Ambrosia Batter is mixed, it may be a little lumpy, but this will disappear as the batter ripens, the same as happens with starter.

The 24-hour aging period of Ambrosia Batter is very important. Like all good things, sourdough foods require time. Twenty-four hours of maturing gives the wild yeast a chance to do its work and develop that unmatchable sourdough flavor. Care must be taken to insure that Ambrosia Batter is put in an area where it is between 75° and 80°. Temperatures lower than this are not warm enough to stimulate fast wild yeast growth. The batter will not develop the proper flavor, nor will it have enough active wild yeast in it to work well in a recipe. The palate of a true sourdough lover will never be satisfied with an Ambrosia Batter that has not reached maturity. It just won't have enough tang.

After Ambrosia Batter "works" for 24 hours, it's ready for use in any of the recipes contained in this part of the book. The first thing you will want to do after the aging period is take the cover off the bowl and smell. The rich fragrance of this freshly fermented medley lets you know why some in days past preferred to drink the stuff instead of eating it. In addition to its distinct aroma you will also notice the Ambrosia Batter has thinned considerably, and any lumps that were present when it was first mixed are gone. This loss of stickiness and smoothing of the batter is due to the action of the wild yeast on the flour and is normal. It's a sign the starter has been laboring to give the batter full savor. If the batter has not thinned, it's probably an indication that the area where it was placed during the 24-hour maturing period was not warm enough or that your starter was in poor condition. See page 26 for sweetening the pot.

Tastes vary a great deal in judging how sour an Ambrosia Batter should be. A batter that has worked for a 24-hour flavoring period gives food made with it a pleasant sourdough taste. Some will deem it too strong, while others will judge it as not being nippy enough. It's strictly a matter of personal opinion.

For those who like a mild sourdough flavor, try aging the Ambrosia Batter for 12 hours instead of the usual 24 hours. This will considerably reduce its sourness. A 12-hour flavoring period will not leave the batter quite as thin as the normal 24-hour period, so you may want to increase slightly the amount of liquids called for in recipes. The pancake recipes especially will most likely need more liquid.

If you're the kind of sourdough enthusiast who likes his lips to pucker when eating hotcakes and biscuits, try ripening the Ambrosia Batter for 36 or even 48 hours. You'll have a batter with enough zip to make a lemon seem sweet.

34

No matter what your preference, bear in mind that the duration of the fermentation process determines the sourness of the batter. The longer you let it age, the stronger it will get.

Patiently fermenting an Ambrosia Batter for future use is the time-honored and by far the best method of cooking with sourdough. All the recipes in this book represent the genuine, old-fashioned manner of using wild yeast. Don't be dismayed, however, if occasionally you run across a recipe which calls for an ingredient such as powdered milk. For the sake of convenience a few recipes have been changed slightly to facilitate their execution, but they all faithfully reproduce the same foods that were eaten in the 1800s and long before.

Griddlecakes

Settlers to the New World brought with them the half-hearted English version of the griddlecake called pan puddings. These were eventually abandoned for what was to evolve into the marvelous American Slapjack. It seems as though Americans have always had an inordinate love for griddlecakes, and little wonder because when they are made with sourdough, they're unbelievably good. One of the finest things that can happen to a rich, frothy, sourdough batter is to turn it into hotcakes. Few of life's pleasures can equal laying into a skyward stack of freshly griddled, honest-to-goodness sourdoughs drowned in butter and hot maple syrup.

Presented here is a collection of hotcakes ranging from the old style American Slapjack to the more modern sourcream cake. All are good, and each deserves to be tried at least once. But before starting any recipes, you should be made aware of some idiosyncrasies peculiar to sourdough griddlecakes.

Unlike the heavy batters resulting from the speciously marketed pre-packaged powders which are supposed to wind up as edible hotcakes, sourdough batter is quite thin. True sourdough griddlecakes are not thick like the oftentimes mushy pancakes made with a mix from a box. Sourdoughs are thin, substantial in texture, and far more enjoyable to eat.

The choicest of wild yeast flapjacks come from a hot, lightly-oiled griddle. The batter should sizzle as it's being poured on. Too much oil on the griddle will make the pancakes crusty and undesirable. When frying, don't use butter because the high heat will cause it to burn. You will also find that making dollar-sized hotcakes produces by far the best results. When sourdough flapjacks are made too large, they generally do not turn out well. Using about a tablespoon of batter per pancake will always give good results.

Sourdough hotcakes can be grilled successfully on most any type of hot, frying surface. Because of their excellent heat conducting qualities, uncoated fry pans and griddles made of cast aluminum or iron work very well. They spread the heat evenly and impart a nice color to the griddlecake, whereas thin-metaled Teflon-coated pans do not.

A problem common to uncoated, heavy cast utensils is sticking, but fortunately this can be overcome with proper "seasoning." Putting a good non-stick finish on a fry pan or griddle is not difficult. To do this use a steel wool pad and scour the frying surface of the utensil until it is completely free from grease, carbon, and old food particles. Put the pan or griddle in a preheated oven at its highest setting and let it bake for 20 minutes. Remove the pan and wipe the grilling surface lightly with a good cooking oil. Allow it to cool completely and set it aside to cure for a day or two. You will find that not only hotcakes griddle very well on properly seasoned metal, but so do eggs. Do not, however, fry meat in a treated pan because it will ruin the seasoning.

This same technique can be successfully used for an electric frying pan. Using a steel wool pad, clean the pan carefully. Heat it to its highest setting and wipe it with a very small amount of oil. Then turn it off. Let it sit for a day before using.

As implausible as it may seem, the way to keep a well-seasoned pan in perfect condition is never to wash it. When soap and water touch a cured frying surface, the fragile glaze is damaged. Nevertheless a pan can be cleaned very satisfactorily without destroying its nonstick qualities by using salt and oil as a scrubbing cleanser. With a teaspoon each of salt and oil, rub the pan with a paper towel. Any food will be quickly and easily removed. Remove the salt-oil cleaning mixture from the pan with another paper towel. The more a pan is used and then cleaned in this way, the better its non-stick qualities become. Omelet pans also work extremely well when cared for in this manner.

One of the pleasing peculiarities of wild yeast cookery is what happens to a hotcake batter when frozen. Most foods deteriorate, but sourdough batter actually improves. The wild yeast seems to respond very favorably to an icy respite of a few days or several weeks. It becomes more tangy and the ingredients of the mix are better combined for improved flavor. If ever there is any batter left over from a sourdough hotcake breakfast, freeze it for future use. When you eventually want to use it, just let it thaw and work for an hour or two in a warm place. Should it be too strong for your taste, adding ¼ teaspoon of baking soda will reduce the sourness.

The American Slapjack

This country really did not have a homegrown cookbook until 1796 when Amelia Simmons had her modest work of 47 pages published. Under the title *American Cookery*, it was first in offering guidance to the use of such indigenous foods as corn and potatoes. This humble compilation was likewise the first to make mention of America's own pancake, the Slapjack. The recipe given here faithfully reproduces this favorite of early American fare.

Unlike some of the griddlecake recipes in this book, the American Slapjack contains no chemical leaveners of any kind. Although they are not bad in themselves, baking powder and bicarbonate of soda do lessen slightly the flavor produced by the long maturing period of Ambrosia Batter. American Slapjacks have the wonderful flavor of an unrepressed, newly-fermented wild yeast. This is the pancake for those who want the full rich flavor of sourdough in all its glory and savor.

American Slapjacks require more time than most sourdough hotcakes. In the early days this presented no problem because the lady of the house was usually up well before the rest of the family. Today, with our faster pace of living, these griddlecakes might present difficulty if it's a quick breakfast you want. Try making them on a Saturday or Sunday morning when you are not rushed. Once the Ambrosia Batter has aged for 24 hours, American Slapjacks require about an hour to re-ferment after they are mixed.

1 recipe Ambrosia Batter — see page 31. ¼ cup honey
1 egg   2 Tablespoons melted butter
½ cup milk   ½ teaspoon salt

Mix the egg, milk, honey, butter and salt in a two-quart bowl. Add the Ambrosia Batter and beat rapidly for about one minute to mix and aerate the batter. Cover and set aside in a very warm place (85° to 110°) for 45 to 90 minutes. This will cause the batter to ferment again and become light and bubbly. After the refermentation period, move the batter very carefully to the griddle so as to avoid knocking out any of the leavening gas. Ladle carefully and fry on a lightly greased griddle. Makes about 40 dollar-sized hotcakes, enough for 3 or 4.

The secret of successfully bringing this recipe to flavorsome perfection is finding a spot warm enough to re-ferment the batter rapidly. Provided that it is not above 120°, an oven on a setting of WARM is the ideal place. Remember to ladle the batter with great care once it has become foamy. The presence of the gas bubbles is what makes the pancakes light. When directions are followed carefully, American Slapjacks are the lightest of all the sourdough griddlecakes and have the best sourdough flavor.

Flannel Cakes

Flannel cakes are old-fashioned griddlecakes, which generally were made with cornmeal. The somewhat unusual name of this hotcake was derived from the now archaic usage of the word "flannel" which a century ago meant "soft and warm." Flannel cakes were best made in true sourdough fashion as the following recipe of 1850—1860 vintage attests:

Take & heat a pint of sweet milk, & into it put a piece of butter the size of a small egg. Let it melt, then add a pint of cold milk & the well-beaten yolks of four fresh eggs. Find a cool place & put the egg whites there. Also put in a teaspoon of salt, four tablespoonfuls of homemade yeast, & sufficient flour & Indian corn meal to make a stiff batter. Let stand overnight near the fire. Before baking, add the beaten whites. Bake like any other griddlecake. Be sure to make the batter stiff enough, for flour & corn meal must not be added after it has risen unless it is allowed to rise again. These, half corn meal & half wheat, are very nice.

Here is the modern version of the above recipe:

42

1 recipe of altered Ambrosia Batter
Use 1 cup starter, ¾ cup white all-purpose flour, ¾ cup yellow corn meal and 1 cup of warm water. Follow the normal Ambrosia Batter procedure as given on page 31.

1 egg, slightly beaten
½ cup milk
¼ cup dry milk
2 Tablespoons melted butter

1 Tablespoon sugar
½ teaspoon salt
¼ teaspoon soda

Combine all the ingredients and mix well. If time allows, let the batter rest for 30 minutes in a very warm place for improved flavor and a lighter cake. Fry on a hot, lightly greased griddle. For a sharper sourdough flavor, leave out the soda. Makes about 40 small cakes.

From historical accounts we know that flannel cakes were often the breakfast fare of Andrew Jackson, seventh President of the United States. The sometime accompaniment to his favorite hotcake was a famous southern dish, red-eye gravy and ham, which was in part his own invention. The story goes that one day during the First Seminole War the then General Jackson sat down for his noontime repast. Being at times a man of wry humor, he was amused to see that his approaching cook was suffering severe "tremens" and had eyes as red as hot pokers, the result of a grand drunk the night before. Old Hickory jocularly bade him to fry up some ham and make a mess of gravy as red as his eyes. Onlookers heard the remark, and from then on it was red-eye gravy and ham.

43

Whether or not the tale is true, red-eye gravy and ham is delicious. To make it, fry ham with a tablespoon of lard in a hot skillet. Remove the ham when it is well browned, and to the drippings add a small amount of flour to make a roux. Cook the roux until it is light brown. Be sure to scrape the pan carefully to remove all the drippings. This will insure good flavor. Once the roux is cooked to a tan color and butternut aroma, add about 1 cup of water, 1 to 2 crushed cloves, 1 teaspoon each of paprika and sugar, and pepper and salt to taste. Allow the mixture to thicken and reduce by boiling it 2 minutes or so. Serve over ham and, if desired, over flannel cakes for an extra hearty breakfast.

Crumbcakes

Long before the days of refrigeration, people employed rather ingenious methods for preserving their food. One old trick was to coddle eggs for twenty seconds in boiling water and then pack them away in sawdust or bran meal. Mrs. Beeton's book *Household Management*, published in 1859, claimed that eggs could be kept two to three months this way with little ill effect. Fortunately, we have gone beyond the time when three-month-old eggs fried for breakfast are to be considered a delightful comestible.

Notwithstanding their best efforts, our ancestors often wound up with food that had progressed to a point where even their somewhat calloused sensibilities dictated the victual inedible and in need of serious doctoring. Old recipe books abound with instructions on how to use soured milk, dry bread, and old butter. And little wonder, taking into account that food was not nearly so plentiful and readily available in all its forms as it is today.

One such recipe I found of the "don't throw it away" type was for sourdough griddlecakes. It called for stale bread which was bludgeoned with a mallet until fine bread crumbs resulted, and then used as a flour substitute in hotcake batter. The result was griddlecakes of fine flavor and small expense.

This particular recipe for crumbcakes renders griddlecakes much unlike others found in this book. These are quite light and very tender. For best results, serve them immediately as they come from the griddle.

1 recipe of altered Ambrosia Batter
    Use 1 cup starter, 1½ cups fine bread crumbs (available at your supermarket), and 1 cup warm water. Follow the regular Ambrosia Batter aging instructions starting on page 33.
1 egg, slightly beaten   1 Tablespoon sugar
1 cup of milk   ½ teaspoon salt
2 Tablespoons of melted butter   ¼ teaspoon baking soda

You will notice that the altered Ambrosia Batter as given above results in much thicker aged batter than usual. This is normal. Combine all the ingredients and mix well. Add more milk if needed; crumbcake batter must be quite thin or the cakes might turn out soggy. Allow the mixed batter to stand 10 to 15 minutes before using. Fry on a hot, lightly-greased griddle. Small, dollar-sized crumbcakes have the best flavor and texture. Be sure to serve them immediately as they come from the griddle. Makes about 40 small cakes.

Cheechakocakes
(CHEE-chaw-ko-cakes)

When the steamer Portland docked in Seattle on July 17, 1897, with the now fabled "ton of gold" from the Klondike, the remaining summer months brought a flood of men to the North. These were drummers, farmers, doctors, sailors, shopkeepers, and the many others who gave up their professions to join the rush to Alaska, the Yukon, and gold. Many were ill suited for the journey, and all were over-burdened with the wrong equipment. Unscrupulous Seattle merchants had sold them everything from 300-pound "portable stoves" to as much as 5,000 pounds of bulky stores and equipment. As Bill Speidel points out in his amusing book *Sons of the Profits*, Seattle took time out to mine the miners.

These greenhorns were called Cheechakos (Indian for newly arrived) by the established, resident sourdoughs. It wasn't until a tyro had remained in the North long enough to see the Yukon River freeze over and then break-up in the spring that he could be classified as a sourdough. If he was a truly exceptional fellow he might further be honored with a colorful handle such as Slivers Perry, Windy Smith, Cockeyed Joe, Hamgreese Jimmy, or Snuff Box Olsen.

Despite their ignorance, Cheechakos certainly left their imprint on Alaska and the Yukon.

One of the things they did was amend the making of the much-revered sourdough griddlecake. Packed in the provisions of all Cheechakos was a tin of baking powder. To the old-time sourdough, baking powder was a sacrilegious artifice. His bubbly pot was all he needed to make his flapjacks and certainly not some infernal "yeast powder." But here the Cheechako took the best of the old and some of the new. Using sourdough starter as a base he added a pinch of baking powder to his hotcake batter, just enough to lighten his griddlecakes and make the sourdough flavor milder.

The Cheechakocake was and is today a good pancake for the sourdough neophyte. It has the distinctive flavor of sourdough but in just the right amount to please the palate of a new sourdough fan. These griddlecakes are quick and easy to prepare and will surely please all who partake of them.

1 recipe Ambrosia Batter—See page 31.
1 egg, slightly beaten   1 Tablespoon sugar
½ cup milk   ½ teaspoon salt
¼ cup dry milk   ½ teaspoon baking powder
1 Tablespoon melted butter

Combine all the ingredients and mix well. Let stand for ten to fifteen minutes before using. The baking powder will cause a slight foaming action in the batter. Fry dollar-sized (1 tablespoon of batter) on a hot, lightly greased griddle. Makes about 40 small hotcakes, enough for 3 or 4.

Buckwheats

The name buckwheat is somewhat of a misnomer considering that it isn't wheat at all but rather the seed of a plant which bears some small resemblance to wheat grain. First introduced to Europe by the Moors, it came to be known as Saracen wheat. Acceptance was rapid because of its ability to withstand unfavorable weather and its need for little care.

In this country buckwheat has long been held in high regard as a choice pancake ingredient. Being coarsely ground, dark in color and with just a hint of bitterness, buckwheat has a pleasingly uncivilized flavor. If you appreciate the taste of whole ground, unbolted grains, buckwheats surely will be a favorite of yours. These battercakes are enough to cause anyone to ply his fork with alacrity.

1 recipe altered Ambrosia Batter
    Use 1 cup of starter, 1 cup of buckwheat flour, ½ cup of white flour and 1 cup of warm water. Follow the normal Ambrosia Batter aging instructions starting on page 33.

1 egg, separated
½ cup milk
¼ cup dry milk
2 Tablespoons sugar

2 Tablespoons butter, melted
½ teaspoon salt
¼ teaspoon baking soda

Combine all the ingredients but the egg white. Mix very thoroughly. Allow the batter to rest 20 minutes. Beat the egg white until it peaks and then gently fold it into the batter. Fry dollar-sized cakes on a hot lightly greased griddle. Makes approximately 40 small cakes.

Although the flavor is somewhat strong, buckwheats go very well with blackstrap molasses. A brace of buckwheats so consumed will stand anyone in good stead the whole day through.

Maplecakes

Folks up in Vermont and Maine are great lovers of fine griddlecakes, and this would seem only right since the choicest of all condiments to accompany sourdough cakes is their local product, pure maple syrup. The rich goodness of sugar-maple syrup is absolutely unsurpassed as an addition to a hot stack of flapjacks.

Indians were the first to discover the sweetness of maple sap. They collected it in wooden vessels and added hot rocks to the sap, causing it to boil and reduce. Seeing this, the early settlers were not long in adopting boiled maple as a main part of their diet. For over two hundred years it was the primary sweetener used in the northeastern part of the country and this being the case, it was only natural that it find its way into sourdough griddlecakes.

As it was one hundred years ago in the back areas of Vermont and Maine, the recipe given here calls for maple syrup as the sole sweetening agent for the pancake batter itself. These cakes are rich in flavor and perfect for those who relish the taste of true maple. Although genuine maple syrup is on the expensive side, indulge yourself at least once and make these griddlecakes the old-fashioned, authentic way with real maple syrup. Don't wince too much at the price because it takes about thirty-five gallons of sap to make one gallon of syrup.

Once a tin of the real thing has been purchased, there are certain precautions you will want to take to insure it stays in good condition. Here are two tips on what to do: Always store maple syrup in a dry cool place in small containers, preferably of glass. Once a gallon tin has been opened, transfer the syrup to glass jars or bottles. Second, if maple syrup ferments slightly or forms a white cloud on top, you can restore it to full flavor by straining it through a sieve lined with cheesecloth or a paper towel and heating it to a full rolling boil. Skim the foam as it forms, then pour the syrup into hot sterilized jars or bottles and store.

1 recipe Ambrosia Batter—See page 31.
1 egg, separated   ½ teaspoon salt
½ cup milk   ½ teaspoon pure vanilla extract
¼ cup pure maple syrup   Pinch of allspice
2 Tablespoons melted butter

50

Combine all the ingredients except the egg white and beat thoroughly for 1 minute. Set the batter aside and beat the egg white until it forms peaks. Gently fold the egg white into the batter. Fry the cakes, dollar-sized, on a lightly oiled, hot griddle. Serve immediately with plenty of real maple syrup and dairy butter. Makes about 40 small cakes.

You may want to eat these biscuit fashion as they did in the old days by dipping the rolled cake directly into hot syrup.

Another fine way of eating maplecakes is with Apple-Maple Sauce. To make this, put 1½ cups of maple syrup in a pan and bring it to a gentle, rolling boil. Add 1 cup of diced, hard, tart apples, 1 teaspoon lemon juice, and ½ teaspoon cinnamon. Cook until the apples are tender. Serve hot over the cakes.

Oaten Cakes

As a youngster I had a predilection for accumulating chips of paper that some refer to as stamp collecting. Aiding me in my avocation was my marvelous Grandmother Williams. She was an assiduous collector of all manner of things, including stamps and coins. When I was ten or eleven years old she gave me a bundle of old letters for my newly started collection. Recently when the occasion arose for me to review the remains of my long since abandoned hobby, I again found that stack of old envelopes, many of which still contained their original letters. While the stamps were of little monetary value, the letters themselves have provided many moments of interesting reading.

I found the recipe for "Oaten Cakes" and a novel method for starting a sourdough pot in one old letter posted March 2, 1897. Mrs. Farger's procedure for launching a homemade yeast pot was as follows:

Boil six large potatoes in three pints of water. Tie a handful of hops in a small muslin bag and boil with the potatoes; when thoroughly cooked, drain the water on enough flour to make a thin batter. Add the potatoes mashed, also a half a teacup of sugar, half a tablespoon of ginger, and two of salt. Let stand in a warm place until it has thoroughly risen, then put it in a large-mouthed jug & cork tightly; set away in a cool place. The jug should be scalded before putting in the yeast.

I'm somewhat skeptical as to the credibility of the preceding sourdough starting procedure, but Mrs. Farger's oaten cakes are certainly very good. Presented here is an updated version of her original recipe which you will find to be delicious.

1 recipe altered Ambrosia Batter
  Use 1 cup starter, 1½ cups of rolled oats and 1 cup warm water. Follow the normal
  Ambrosia Batter aging instructions on page 33.

1 egg, slightly beaten	2 Tablespoons sugar
1 Tablespoon butter, melted	½ teaspoon salt
¼ cup powdered milk	¼ teaspoon soda

Before adding any ingredients to altered Ambrosia Batter, use an electric or hand mixer to beat the batter for 2 to 3 minutes. This smooths it and improves its griddling qualities. Add the rest of the ingredients and mix. You will find that oaten batter is thicker and lumpier than other sourdough hotcake batters. The lumps disappear when the cake is griddled. Fry on a hot, lightly greased griddle. Oaten cakes are best when made dollar-size. Makes about 40 cakes.

By the way, for oatmeal that would make even a Scotsman take notice, try this method. Put 1 cup of rolled oats (instant or long cooking), 3 cups of water, ½ tablespoon butter, ¼ teaspoon salt, and ¼ teaspoon cinnamon in a double boiler. Cover and cook all night at low heat. The next morning, turn up the heat and cook for 10 minutes if the porridge needs to be thickened. Serve with brown sugar and milk or half and half. You'll find this to be the creamiest oatmeal you have ever eaten, and far more satisfying than the customary air-puffed cereal from boxes.

Crêpes

Crêpes are the thin, lacy pancake of France and are not ordinarily made with sourdough. Nevertheless, crêpes made with a wild yeast batter have a better and far more interesting flavor than the plain, traditional mixture of flour, milk, and eggs. You will find this recipe will give you crêpes suitable for a wide range of uses. They can be stuffed with anything from fruits to meat and can be used as a dessert or main entree item.

Crêpes are particularly fun to prepare because the usual method of turning them is by flipping. This is not nearly as hard as it might seem, but you will probably want to practice privately before showing off your expertise in front of family or friends. Use a well-seasoned 6- or 8-inch pan that has sloped sides. Put a small amount of butter into it, enough to lightly coat the bottom, and heat over a medium fire. Pour in the batter and roll it around until the bottom of the pan is covered. Remember that the pancake should be quite thin. When the crêpe is lightly browned on the bottom and dry on the top, shake the pan to insure that the crêpe is not sticking. A rubber spatula is helpful in loosening any recalcitrant cakes. Now grasp the pan at the end of the handle and slide the pancake to and fro, away from and toward you. This should be a flowing, even motion. Add more butter if necessary. After gliding the pancake back and forth a few times for practice, with a firm flick of the wrist, flip the crêpe when it reaches the edge of the pan furthest from you. The crêpe should almost be allowed to slip from the pan before flicking the wrist. Don't be alarmed if the first one or two don't make it back into their proper place; the loss is negligible. In no time you'll be flipping pancakes like a French chef, sailing them high and wide.

For those who eschew theatrics, crêpes can be turned very well without the fanfare of flipping by using a rubber spatula.

½ recipe Ambrosia Batter—See page 31.
4 eggs, beaten
¾ cup milk
½ cup melted butter
¼ cup powdered milk
¼ teaspoon salt

Combine all the ingredients and mix. The batter should have the consistency of cream; add more milk if needed. Flip or turn the crêpes when the bottom is flecked with brown spots. Stir the batter each time before adding it to the fry pan. This helps to keep the crêpe from sticking by keeping the butter mixed with the batter.

Finished crêpes can be folded in four (fan shape) and garnished with powdered sugar and lemon juice. For Crêpes Suzettes, make a sauce of ½ cup orange marmalade, 3 tablespoons of Grand Marnier, 2 tablespoons of butter, 2 tablespoons of sugar, ¼ cup of cognac or good brandy. Mix, simmer for three minutes, and pour over folded crêpes. For traditionalists who must have their crêpes *en flambé*, melt 3 to 4 tablespoons of butter in a large skillet or chafing dish. There should be enough to cover the bottom of the pan completely. Spread the pancakes with orange marmalade mixed with a small amount of cognac or brandy, fold into a fan shape and arrange in the pan. Sprinkle them with 2 tablespoons of sugar mixed with 1 teaspoon freshly shredded orange rind. Heat very gently, turning once, until the pancakes are quite hot. Pour on ¼ cup of brandy, 3 tablespoons of Grand Marnier and heat the liquor. Then light. Whoooosh! Shaking the pan will prolong the flame. Eat as soon as the flames die down.

String o' Thins

String o' thins was the common vernacular of the Old West used to denote a high stack of sourdough cakes. These were usually prepared only at the ranch cookhouse when the hands were home, but an enterprising camp sizzler would sometimes fix them while on the range over a fire of steer chips or corn cobs. Both burned well and produced a fire perfect for flapjack flipping and coffee making.

The unique flavor of the old style string o' thins was brought about by the use of lick (molasses), bacon or salt pork lard, and rough ground flour all mixed with a liberal scoop of well-fermented starter. The molasses added color and a bit of spiciness while the lard and the rough ground flour (laden with bran and wheat germ) gave the cakes a satisfying and full flavor.

String o' thins were served in a manner unlike most sourdough hotcakes. They were made large, stacked high with sweetener layered in between, and then cut in wedges, pie fashion. If you want to try this, griddle 8-inch cakes and as they are made, spread each very generously with a mixture of brown sugar and warm butter. The butter and sugar will melt to make their own syrup. As you fry, keep the string o' thins warm by putting them in a preheated oven at 225°. When you have a stack of cakes 3 to 4 inches high, cut into wedges and serve. Then you had better start all over again because everyone will want more.

The recipe given below is a fine example of Old West camp cooking. It requires the use of whole cracked wheat which you can procure at gourmet or health foods stores.

1 recipe altered Ambrosia Batter.
   Use 1 cup starter, 1 cup all-purpose flour, ½ cup cracked wheat. Follow the normal
   Ambrosia Batter instructions as given on page 31.

1 egg, slightly beaten

¼ cup milk

2 Tablespoons of bacon fat or
   salt pork lard, melted

1 Tablespoon molasses

1 Tablespoon sugar

½ teaspoon salt

¼ teaspoon soda

Combine all the ingredients and mix well. Fry on a hot, lightly greased griddle. Stir the batter frequently to keep the cracked wheat well mixed. String o' thins are also very good if you prefer dollar-sized cakes.

Waffles

Waffles and griddlecakes are closely related, the primary difference being the amount of oil or shortening each type of batter contains. As with crêpes, waffles contain a good portion of butter to keep them from sticking to the cooking surface. This is why a waffle iron generally does not have to be greased. Do, however, make sure that it has been properly seasoned; follow the manufacturer's instructions for this. The extra butter in waffle batter also helps to make the waffles crisp.

The following recipe will give you the same kind of good, wholesome waffles great-grandma used to make over the open fire with her Griswold waffle iron.

1 recipe Ambrosia Batter—See page 31.
2 eggs separated
⅓ cup melted butter
¼ cup milk (more or less, as needed)

1 Tablespoon sugar
½ teaspoon salt

Combine all the ingredients except the egg white. Mix. Beat the egg whites until they form peaks and fold them gently into the batter. Use about ½ cup of batter for a 6-inch waffle iron. Like sourdough hotcakes, sourdough waffles should be griddled on a slightly hotter surface than regular waffles. Sourdough waffles bake in about 6 minutes. Makes about 10 6-inch waffles.

Use your imagination as to condiments: ice cream, fruit syrups, whipped cream, sour cream mixed with brown sugar, or any of the toppings listed under Griddlecake Garnishes.

Sourcream Cakes

Sourcream holds a high place as an ingredient in fine cooking.

Stroganoffs, various sauces, ice cream and salad dressings are all enhanced by its addition. Too few of us, however, consider its use in baking. It imparts a rich, zesty flavor to all baked goods. Try it in cakes, biscuits, and especially bread.

Graduates of the purchased-mix pancake league might find this recipe for sourcream cakes an unusual experience. It's a shame that our much abused taste buds have been so inundated with the vapid, preservative-saturated foods which emanate from those little cardboard boxes. It is difficult at times for us to reacquaint ourselves with that which is fresh, homemade from scratch, and truly excellent. Undoubtedly the consumer trend away from "the housewife's friend," such as the silly merchandising gimmick of Betty Crocker (she must be 100 by now) and other fictional entities, is a good one. You will find sourcream cakes unlike the soggy, mushy pancakes you're most likely used to. They are good old-fashioned cooking at its best.

1 recipe altered Ambrosia Batter
Use 1 cup starter, ¾ cup whole wheat flour, ¾ cup all-purpose white flour and 1 cup warm water. Follow the normal aging procedure for Ambrosia Batter starting on page 33.

1 egg, slightly beaten
½ cup sour cream, warmed
¼ cup milk
2 Tablespoons brown sugar

1 Tablespoon butter, melted
½ teaspoon salt
¼ teaspoon baking powder
1 drop pure vanilla extract

Make sure that the sourcream has been warmed sufficiently so that it is thin. Combine all the ingredients and mix thoroughly. Fry on a lightly greased griddle. Makes approximately 40 small hotcakes.

Griddlecake Garnishes

Although it is really hard to beat the time-honored combination of melted butter and hot maple syrup there are a number of other condiments that go very well with sourdough griddlecakes. Honey or brown sugar mixed with butter are both excellent. Sugared fresh fruits drowned in their own syrup and then stirred with sourcream make delightfully different toppings. And when time allows, try the syrups and sauces listed here. Their use will provide taste adventures which you are sure to enjoy.

Nut Maple Crackle

½ cup water
½ cup walnuts, finely chopped

2 cups maple sugar
(brown sugar may be substituted)

60

Add the water to the maple or brown sugar and boil until it reaches the thread stage (230°-234°). Add the finely chopped walnuts. Serve hot.

Honey Sauce

1 egg
1 cup honey
1 cup hot water

2 Tablespoons butter
½ cup lemon juice
1 teaspoon lemon rind, grated
Pinch of salt

Beat the egg thoroughly. Add the other ingredients in the order given. Cook in a double boiler over gently boiling water for 10 minutes or until thickened slightly. Stir constantly. Serve hot.

Orange Syrup

1 cup light corn syrup
¼ cup frozen orange juice
   concentrate

2 Tablespoons butter
Few grains of salt

Combine the ingredients and heat in a saucepan, stirring frequently. Serve hot.

Burnt Sugar Syrup

½ cup white sugar
½ cup brown sugar
½ cup water

¼ teaspoon vanilla
Few grains salt

Combine sugars and salt. Heat over a medium high heat until melted. Stir constantly to prevent scorching. When the liquid is dark, remove from heat and carefully add water. Sugar syrup sizzles when water is added to it. Add the vanilla. Serve hot.

Spiced Honey Syrup

1 cup honey
1 teaspoon cinnamon
½ teaspoon nutmeg

¼ teaspoon allspice
2 finely chopped almonds

Combine ingredients, heat and serve hot over cakes.

Egg-Cream Sauce

This garnish is somewhat out of the realm of traditional griddlecake or waffle condiments but is truly delicious when poured over a combination of fresh fruits and flapjacks. Cheechakocakes (see page 46) layered with fresh, sugared strawberries and then doused with this sauce make a great dessert.

62

1 cup half & half
2 Tablespoons sugar
Pinch of salt

2 egg yolks
¼ teaspoon vanilla

Scald the half & half in top of a double boiler. Separately combine the egg yolks, sugar, salt and beat slightly. Add the hot half & half to egg mixture and mix thoroughly. Return to the top of the double boiler. Cook over hot (not boiling) water, stirring constantly, until the sauce coats the spoon. Add the vanilla. Serve when the sauce has cooled slightly.

Old-Fashioned Molasses Topping

1 cup molasses
2 Tablespoons butter

2 teaspoons lemon juice

Simmer molasses with butter for approximately 5 minutes. Remove from the fire and slowly stir in lemon juice. Excellent on buckwheats.

Maple-Apple-Spice Sauce

1 cup applesauce
1 cup maple syrup
1 teaspoon lemon juice

¼ teaspoon cinnamon
¼ teaspoon allspice
¼ teaspoon vanilla

Combine applesauce, maple syrup, cinnamon and allspice. If you are using commercially canned applesauce you will want to cook the mixture until it darkens slightly. Home-made applesauce need only be cooked for 2 or 3 minutes. Remove cooked mixture from the fire and stir in the vanilla and lemon juice. This sauce is best when served hot.

Quickbreads

The prodigious assortment of biscuits, griddlecakes, desserts, and breads which can be summoned from the sourdough pot all attest to its versatility. In this section are found the famous sourdough "quick breads." The name applies to the biscuits and kindred breadstuffs which are given an extra kick with the help of the much-maligned baker's friend, baking powder. Sourdough cooks were a long time in accepting baking powder as a part of their ritual, especially the denizens of the far North. Before the Great Rush of 1897, someone started the nasty rumor that baking powder inhibited one's sexual prowess. That did it! An old-timer wouldn't touch the stuff for love or money, and it wasn't until the arrival of the cheechakos that "yeast powder" and "baker's salt" found their rightful place.

The French got hold of the Spanish word *bizcocho* around the time of Louis XIV and changed it to the more recognizable word of today, *biscuit*. An American gold digger couldn't have cared less where the word came from so long as his biscuits were sourdough. In this part of the book we will explore some of the great old-time biscuit and quick bread recipes used more than one hundred years ago. You will become familiar with such colorful names as bannock, snow biscuit, and billycan bread. Also included is a recipe for the best blueberry muffins you ever ate.

Before going into our various recipes, a word is needed as to how light and flaky biscuits are made. As with any type of biscuit, the sourdough variety has a certain way of being put together so that success is insured.

The most important aspect of all good biscuit making is the manner in which the flour and other dry ingredients are combined with the shortening at the time specified by the recipe. The best method of blending the shortening with the dry ingredients of the recipe is by using a procedure known as "cutting in." If you are new to the sometimes confusing art of baking, cutting-in refers to the use of two small knives employed in a cutting motion to break the shortening into small pieces and mix them with the flour. The resulting mixture should have a mealy, inconsistent texture. The shortening makes the biscuit tender while the mealy consistency aids in producing flakiness.

Another term the novice baker will want to become familiar with is "kneading." It refers to the final mixing process a biscuit dough goes through. When a dough has been mixed to the point where it is too stiff to be stirred by hand, it is taken from the bowl and put on a bread board which has been sprinkled with flour. This is where the final mixing (kneading) takes place. Using the hands, the dough is shaped into a ball. With the palm of the hand at the top of the ball, the dough is pushed down and forward. The dough is not pushed down so hard as to make it stick to the board or hands. A light touch is used to flatten it. The hands are next cupped around the dough at its widest point and it is reshaped into a ball. The dough is then rotated a quarter turn and pressed down again. The procedure of shaping, pressing, rotating, and reshaping, is repeated for 30 seconds at an even, steady pace. This method of kneading applies to all the biscuit recipes in this section. Kneading dough for 30 seconds is referred to as light kneading. Bread requires much more vigorous and longer kneading, as we will discuss later. Biscuits, however, turn out best when kneaded lightly, just enough to help mix the ingredients.

Probably the most irritating feature that can be found in a cookbook of any kind is the use of a technical term such as "cutting in" and then not explaining what is meant. To avoid this problem, a glossary of cooking terms has been provided in the back of the book. It contains a clear explanation of all the words peculiar to sourdough and its uses.

Brown Biscuit

Brown biscuit is an old sourdough recipe for whole wheat biscuits. It was a mainstay of western fare long before barbed wire ranged the great expanse west of the Mississippi and has the strong, hearty taste of whole wheat with a hint of bacon flavor.

1 recipe Ambrosia Batter—See instructions on page 31.
2 cups whole wheat flour
½ cup hardened bacon fat
2 Tablespoons brown sugar

2 teaspoons baking powder
½ teaspoon salt

In a 2-quart bowl, blend the dry ingredients: flour, brown sugar, baking powder and salt. Cut in the ½ cup hardened bacon fat. Add the Ambrosia Batter and stir vigorously until the mixture can no longer be stirred by hand. Turn the dough onto a lightly floured board and knead for 20 to 30 seconds, about 15 strokes. Shape the dough into a ball and handling it lightly, flatten it out to a thickness of ¾ inch. Cut the biscuits with a floured cutter, being careful not to twist the dough as the cut is made. (A small juice can with both ends cut out works well as a biscuit cutter.) Place the cut biscuits on a baking pan sprinkled with the corn meal. If biscuits with crusty sides are desired, space them one inch apart. For biscuits with a brown top and soft sides, space them so they are touching. Brush the biscuits with the melted bacon fat. Allow the fat to harden and then cover the biscuits loosely with a clear film such as Saran Wrap. Place the biscuits in a warm place (at least 75°) and allow to rise for 2 hours before baking. Bake at 425° for 15 minutes or until the crust is an even brown and the inside is light, flaky and dry.

These biscuits are best when they are finger-burning hot, right out of the oven, and served with plenty of butter and fireweed honey.

Johnnycake

In the days of Colonial America the most popular kind of bread utilizing the corn of the New World was hoecake. Using unleavened cornmeal dough in the shape of a fat griddlecake, it was baked over an open fire on the flat of a hoe. Hoecake was eventually supplanted by the much more delicious and savory johnnycake (journey cake) which was made with the use of homemade "barm," otherwise known as sourdough.

Johnnycake is a fine sourdough cornbread not having the usual gritty, crumbly texture of today's cornbread. The secret of good johnnycake is to mix starter, water, and cornmeal together, and let it age and ripen for 24 hours. This softens the cornmeal and results in a much better cornbread. Another advantage of johnnycake is that you have the option of making it as heavy or as light as you wish.

In the following recipe the only concession made to progress is the powdered milk. All else remains the same as it was years ago. You will also notice that it contains no "tartaric and soda."

1 recipe altered Ambrosia Batter
    Use 1 cup starter, 1½ cups cornmeal and 1 cup warm water. Follow the normal Ambrosia Batter aging instructions starting on page 33.

2 eggs, slightly beaten   3 Tablespoons sugar
⅓ cup powdered milk   1 teaspoon salt
¼ cup melted butter

Combine all the ingredients and mix thoroughly. Grease a heavy skillet (8-inch or 9-inch are good sizes) and flour it, discarding the excess flour. For **heavy** cornbread: Pour the batter into the skillet and bake immediately at 450° for approximately 25 minutes. For **light** cornbread: (This procedure is a little tricky, but the extra effort is well worth the end result.) Pour the batter into the skillet and place it in an oven which has been preheated at the lowest setting of "warm." (The oven must not be above 120°). This puts the batter in a warm area where it again can start to ferment. The length of time the batter is allowed to re-ferment (up to 1 hour) determines the lightness of the johnnycake. If the lightest possible cornbread is desired, ferment the batter for about an hour. Less than that amount of time will yield correspondingly heavier johnnycake. In any case, at the first signs of falling, bake immediately. Bake at 450° for approximately 25 to 30 minutes or until the crust is nicely browned.

Billycan Bread

The Gold Rush prospectors of the North were not very particular about the way they threw their billycan bread together. Using a small billycan as a mixing container and baking pan all in one, they would feel their way along, natural-like, combining ingredients at random and certainly never measuring any. The potion might be ruined if it was "humored" too much.

The assembly instructions for your billycan bread follow a more particular procedure than any sourdough would use, but the results are just as good. You will find billycan bread to be tangy with the taste of sourdough.

1 recipe of altered Ambrosia Batter

    Use 1 cup starter, 1 cup all-purpose flour, ½ cup whole wheat flour and 1 cup warm water. Follow the regular Ambrosia Batter aging directions starting on page 33. For this recipe the starter must be fresh. See the instructions for sweetening the pot on page 26.

⅓ cup powdered milk

¼ cup melted butter

1 Tablespoon sugar

2 teaspoons baking powder

½ teaspoon salt

Combine all the ingredients and mix very well. Butter an 8-inch or 9-inch heavy skillet and flour it, discarding the excess flour. Pour in the billycan bread batter. Place in an oven that has been preheated on the lowest setting of "warm." The temperature must not be higher than 120°. Turn off the oven and place a pan of boiling water in the bottom of it. Shut the oven door and let the billycan bread rise for 30 minutes. (The boiling water helps to keep the top of the batter from crusting as it rises.) At the end of the 30-minute raising period, set the oven to 400° and bake for 35 to 40 minutes or until the bread has a nice brown crust on it. Allow to cool before serving.

If you especially enjoy your sourdough bread really sour, billycan bread can be made entirely without baking powder, which takes away sourness. Follow the same recipe as above but make the following adjustments. Leave out the baking powder and add an extra tablespoon of sugar. This gives the wild yeast more to feed on. Allow the billycan bread batter to rise for about 60 instead of 30 minutes. Bake as usual. The resulting bread will pin your ears back.

Bannock

Since it is made with oats, it isn't surprising that bannock is of Scottish origin. In Scotland there was a type of bannock for every imaginable situation. There was "cryin' bannock" for the midwife, a hard "teetin' bannock" for the "childer" cutting teeth, and a salt bannock (bonnack salainn) which was said to cause a young girl to dream of her future husband if she ate it on Allhallows Eve (Halloween).

Yankee cooks were not long in adopting bannock as one of their favorite biscuits. American sourdough bannock is quite unlike its Scottish cousin, however, in that it's more like bread than biscuit. It has a nice crust, is chewy, and has a bit of a crunch to it.

1 recipe altered Ambrosia Batter
  Use 1 cup starter, 1½ cups rolled oats and 1 cup warm water. Follow the normal Ambrosia Batter aging instructions starting on page 33.

¾ cup all-purpose flour   1 Tablespoon molasses
¼ cup melted butter   2 teaspoons baking powder
2 Tablespoons sugar   ½ teaspoon salt

Mix the Ambrosia Batter with the melted butter, sugar, molasses, baking powder, and salt. Add the flour and mix until the dough can no longer be stirred. Turn onto a floured bread board. Knead the dough for 1 minute, approximately 30 to 40 strokes.

Shape the dough into a ball and flatten it to a thickness of ¾-inch. Cut the bannock in squares with a knife, being careful not to twist the dough as the cut is being made. Place the biscuits 1 inch apart on a baking pan sprinkled with cornmeal. Brush with melted butter. Allow the butter to harden and then cover the pan loosely with a clear film such as Saran Wrap. Place the bannock in a warm area (at least 75°) and raise for 2 hours. Bake in a hot oven of 425° for 25 minutes or until nicely browned.

Snow Biscuits

Out west the cowboys used to refer to husband-hunting females as nester gals. True to the old proverb that the way to a man's heart is through his stomach, a nester gal would.entice her beau with sumptuous meals. Included in these feasts were sourdough snow biscuits, as white and light as new-fallen powder.

1 recipe of Ambrosia Batter; however, use pastry flour instead of all-purpose. Follow the normal Ambrosia Batter aging directions starting on page 33.

1¾ cups pastry flour

½ cup (1 cube) butter

2 Tablespoons sugar

2 teaspoons baking powder

½ teaspoon salt

In a 2-quart bowl, assemble and mix all the dry ingredients: pastry flour, sugar, baking powder, and salt. Cut in the butter. Add the Ambrosia Batter and stir vigorously until the mixture can no longer be stirred by hand. Turn the dough onto a lightly floured board and knead for 20 to 30 seconds, approximately 15 strokes. Shape the dough into a ball and handling it lightly, flatten it out to a thickness of ¾ inch. Cut the biscuits with a floured biscuit cutter. Be careful not to twist the dough as it's being cut. Arrange the biscuits close together on a buttered cookie sheet. Brush with melted butter. When the butter has hardened, cover the biscuits loosely with a clear film such as Saran Wrap. Set aside in a warm place (at least 75°) to rise for 2 hours before baking. Bake at 425° for 15 minutes or until the top crust is an even brown and the inside is light, flaky and dry.

Strawberry shortcake made with snow biscuits make an excellent dessert. Add an extra tablespoon or two of sugar and follow the regular directions. The zest of the sourdough flavor goes perfectly with strawberries.

Blueberry Muffins

Sourdough makes incomparable blueberry muffins. You can also make this recipe without the blueberries if you wish. With or without them, serve these muffins with lots of butter and jam. They are perfect for breakfast.

1 recipe altered Ambrosia Batter
    Use 1 cup starter, 1¼ cups all purpose flour, 1 cup water, ¼ cup toasted wheat germ.
¾ cup blueberries, well drained if canned
1 egg, slightly beaten   ½ cup brown sugar
¾ cup whole wheat flour   2 teaspoons baking powder
⅓ cup powdered milk   ½ teaspoon salt
¼ cup butter

Mix the egg with the Ambrosia Batter. Separately, combine all the dry ingredients and then cut in the butter. Add the Ambrosia Batter and stir only enough to wet the ingredients. The batter should have a lumpy, rough-textured appearance. Very gently mix in the blueberries. Pour the completed batter into a buttered and floured muffin tin, filling each cup ¾ full. Place muffin tin in an oven which has been preheated at a setting of "warm." Allow the muffins to rise for 15 minutes, remove from the oven and reset it to 400°. When the oven is hot, bake the muffins for 25 to 30 minutes.

Desserts

Though it may seem unlikely, sourdough and desserts have long been boon companions. The tanginess of sourdough goes well with fruit, and oldtime cooks often had recourse to the sourdough pot as a source of duffs, pies, pandowdies, and other cheer. Even cake tastes better when seasoned with a scoop of well-fermented starter.

Vanilla Custard Ice Cream

Since several of the recipes found in this section are perfect when served with homemade ice cream, here is an ice-cream recipe that will rival any. It was found on the instruction circular that came with the Eskimo hand crank ice-cream makers around 1910.

2 cups heavy cream
¾ cup sugar
¼ cup sourcream

4 eggs, beaten
1 Tablespoon pure vanilla extract
1/8 teaspoon salt

Mix and scald the cream and sourcream. Pour off one cup of the cream/sourcream mixture and set it aside. In a double boiler, mix the remaining cream/sourcream mixture with the eggs, salt, and sugar. Stir constantly and cook until the mixture coats the spoon. Avoid overcooking; cook just enough for the mixture to thicken slightly. Remove from the stove and strain. To the cooked custard, add the vanilla and 1 cup cooled cream/sourcream and stir. Put the completed ice-cream mix in the refrigerator to chill thoroughly before freezing it to make ice cream. Follow the regular procedure for freezing ice cream, but stir the mix slowly at first. This will avoid giving the ice cream a buttery texture.

Cherry Pandowdy

When stoves were still being stoked with wood, a newly-married wife would often find herself admonished with such maxims as, "Kissing wears out; cookery don't." Pandowdies were one of the devices a good wife used to make sure her man was happy. They have an aroma when baked that would tempt a saint. Few pleasures of the table can surpass this delicacy.

The filling:

4 cups tart, pitted pie cherries
1¼ cups sugar
½ cup cold water

1 Tablespoon corn starch
¼ teaspoon salt

Mix the cherries and sugar together. Pour into a buttered baking dish. Separately mix the water, corn starch, and salt; pour over the sugared cherries. Dot the mixture with butter and cover. Bake for 15 minutes at 425°. Remove from the oven and chill the baked fruit.

If you're short of time, any canned filling can be substituted for the homemade kind.

The crust:

½ recipe Ambrosia Batter—See page 31.

1 cup pastry flour	1 teaspoon baking powder
¼ cup butter	¼ teaspoon salt
1 Tablespoon sugar	1/8 teaspoon pure vanilla extract

In a 2-quart bowl, assemble and mix all the dry ingredients: pastry flour, sugar, baking powder and salt. Cut in the butter. Add the Ambrosia Batter and vanilla and stir vigorously until the mixture can no longer be stirred by hand. Turn the dough onto a lightly floured board and knead for 20 to 30 seconds, approximately 15 strokes. Flatten the dough to a thickness of ½-inch and place it over the chilled fruit. Brush with butter. When the butter has hardened, cover the crust loosely with a clear film such as Saran Wrap. Set aside in a warm place (at least 75°) to rise for 2 hours before baking. Bake for 35 to 40 minutes at 425°.

Rich Chocolate Cake
(3 layers)

It is lamentable that boxed imposters have largely replaced the fine skills of homemade cake making. Our great grandmothers and those before them were happily not subjected to the debauchery of today's modern supermarket and were consequently marvelous cake makers. Many used a sizable scoop of sourdough starter in their recipes to make their creations all the more flavorful and moist. The following recipe is of the old-fashioned kind with a variety of different flavors in combination: vanilla, coffee, real butter, lots of bitter chocolate and, lastly, sourdough. If you follow this recipe carefully, it will easily be the best chocolate cake you have ever eaten.

1st Step:

1½ cups cake flour
⅓ cup powdered milk

1 teaspoon baking soda
½ teaspoon salt

Combine and mix these dry ingredients. Set aside.

2nd Step:

1 cup well fermented starter. Replenish the starter the same as for Ambrosia Batter. See page 32.

1 cup strong, black coffee, cooled
1 teaspoon pure vanilla extract

Combine and mix. Set aside.

3rd Step:

4 oz. (4 squares) bitter chocolate

½ cup butter (1 cube)

2 cups sugar

3 eggs, separated

Melt the chocolate in a double boiler on low heat. Cream the butter, add the sugar to this and beat rapidly until fluffy. Beat the egg yolks into this mixture one at a time. Next add the melted chocolate and beat rapidly for 30 seconds. Continue to beat rapidly and at 15-second intervals, add ½ cup of the cake flour mixture and then ½ cup of the sour-dough/coffee mixture. Proceed until all three mixtures are thoroughly combined and the batter is smooth. Set aside. Beat the egg whites (make sure the beaters are clean) until they form peaks. Fold the beaten egg whites gently into the cake batter. Pour the completed cake batter into three cake pans which have been lined on the bottom with waxed paper and buttered on the sides. Bake in a preheated oven at 350° for 30 to 40 minutes. When the cake has shrunk away from the sides of the pan and springs back when lightly touched at the center, it is done. Remove the cake from the oven and cool.

For a truly excellent frosting to go with your chocolate sourdough cake, try this icing.

1 6-oz. pkg. (1 cup) semi-
 sweet chocolate morsels
⅔ cup brown sugar, firm-
 ly packed
1 3-oz. pkg. cream cheese,
 softened

½ teaspoon vanilla
1 teaspoon cinnamon
Dash salt
1 egg yolk
1 cup heavy cream, whipped

Melt the chocolate over hot, not boiling, water. Meanwhile, beat the sugar, cream cheese, vanilla, cinnamon, and salt together until creamy; beat in the egg yolk; next, stir in the melted chocolate; finally, fold in the whipped cream. Cover and refrigerate until thick, about 1 hour. Frost.

Spicy Fritters

These are so good you can eat them like doughnuts.

1 cup starter. Replenish the starter pot the same as for Ambrosia Batter.
See page 32.

1 cup all-purpose flour

½ cup sugar

1 egg

1 teaspoon baking powder

½ teaspoon nutmeg

¼ cup powdered milk

2 Tablespoons melted butter

½ teaspoon salt

½ teaspoon allspice

¼ teaspoon cinnamon

Combine all the ingredients and mix well. Cover and set aside in a warm place to rise for 2 hours. Gently scoop out with a large spoon and fry in fat which has been heated to 375°. Place fried fritters on absorbent paper. These may be dusted with sugar or eaten as is.

Green Apple Duff

In their written accounts, sourdoughs would occasionally mention how they would make a duff when a bottle of Hudson's Bay rum was at hand. This was the old-fashioned steamed pudding filled with raisins, wild fruits, apples, and anything else that was available at the time. Masked with rum sauce, it was delicious.

To make a duff, you will need a large pot with a cover. Duffs are steamed over boiling water

while resting in a cradle. To make a cradle, use heavy wire and bend it into a "U" shape so that there are 3 inches between the bottom of the pot and the cradle. The ends of the wire are hooked over the edge of the pot to hold them.

After 4 or 5 wires have been bent into shape, complete the cradle by fitting a piece of metal screen into it. This will hold the duff while it is being steamed and will prevent the wires from cutting into it.

The crust:

½ recipe Ambrosia Batter — See page 31.
1 cup all purpose flour   1 Tablespoon sugar
¼ cup cooking oil   ½ teaspoon salt

Mix the Ambrosia Batter, ¾ cup of the flour, cooking oil, sugar and salt. When the mixture can no longer be stirred by hand, turn the dough onto a bread board sprinkled with the remaining ¼ cup flour. Knead well. Place the finished dough on a piece of waxed paper. Roll out to a thickness of ¼-inch. The shape the rolled dough should take is dependent upon the size of the pot you are going to steam the duff in. Trim the edges, saving the trimmings. Once the dough is rolled out to the size you want it, cover with another piece of waxed paper and set it aside.

To make the filling:

2 cups finely diced tart
  green apples
¾ cup sugar
¼ cup raisins
2 Tablespoons melted butter

1 teaspoon grated lemon rind
  Grate only the yellow
  from the rind.
¼ teaspoon allspice

Combine and mix the ingredients.

To put the duff together, remove the top layer of waxed paper and spread the dough with the fruit mixture. Spread the fruit mixture, leaving a margin of 1 inch around the edge of the dough. This will help in sealing the duff so that juices don't escape while it's being steamed. Using the waxed paper backing to assist you, roll the dough up in jellyroll fashion, peeling off the waxed paper as you go. Seal the ends and the seam of the duff, using the dough trimmings if necessary. Place the completed roll in the freezer for a few minutes. This will firm the duff. While the roll is chilling, start the steaming-pot boiling. When the duff has hardened to the point where it can be handled easily, wrap it in a clean cloth with the seam of the dough facing up. Place it in the cradle. Make sure the water is boiling rapidly. Cover. Steam for 2 to 2½ hours, putting in more boiling water as necessary.

Once the duff has cooked, take it out and run it briefly under cold water. This hint from Mrs. Beeton's book *Household Management* helps to separate the duff from the cloth. Once the duff is unwrapped, it's ready to be served. Do not serve the end pieces, and accompany the duff with plenty of homemade ice cream or serve it with the following:

Green Apple Duff Sauce

1 cup cold water
¾ cup sugar
2 teaspoons corn starch

1 Tablespoon lemon juice
1 teaspoon cinnamon

Combine all ingredients and mix well. Bring to a boil and serve hot over the duff.

SOURDOUGH BREAD

Along with hot dogs and hamburgers, sourdough bread is 100 per cent American. We invented true sourdough bread and elevated it to its rightful place as a gastronomical delicacy. If you were to carefully peruse Escoffier's cookbook or any of the other great European works, you would find nary a mention of sourdough or the wonderful bread made with it. In fact, European visitors to 19th century America were appalled to find us eating "soured breads." They considered sourdough bread to have poor flavor, a contributing factor to ill health and the primary cause of dyspepsia (heartburn). How mistaken they were!

You should be made aware of the fact that sourdough bread baking comprises a good deal more than simply the variety which comes from San Francisco. There are many fragrant, mouth-watering loaves that can be conjured from your sourdough pot. Almost any kind of bread can be made with sourdough, although a little more care and understanding is necessary than with bread made with ordinary, commercial yeast. By now you will have had a chance to use sourdough in griddlecakes, biscuits, and desserts. Your experience will be of great value to you in sourdough bread baking. This section is at the back of the book for that reason.

Sourdough bread making requires a mite of an artist's touch because it's the most difficult aspect of sourdough cookery. To help you bake real, honest-to-goodness sourdough bread without the use of any commercial yeast or baking soda, the next several pages contain valuable information which you will want to read carefully. If you are an experienced bread maker, you will still want to read these instructions with care. They will teach you all the tricks needed to produce sourdough bread which rises well and has that great sourdough flavor.

Keep in mind that the sourdough bread you bake will be wholly unlike the dainty, cake-like deceptions to which you have become accustomed. Sourdough bread is honest bread with a heavier, rougher and more uncivilized texture. It might take a loaf or two for you to become accustomed to the real thing, but once you do, you'll never again be completely satisfied with the doughy pap sold in grocery stores.

Flour

In bread making the kind of wheat flour utilized is quite important. The type you will want to use is one that has a high gluten content. Don't let the word gluten throw you. It is simply a baker's term meaning the protein found in wheat flour. When a bread dough is kneaded, the protein (gluten) in the flour becomes elastic and stretchy. Bread making can be likened to blowing up a balloon. As a wild or commercial yeast ferments, it gives off gas (CO_2) and a kneaded, stretchy dough becomes raised by catching and holding it. The more gluten a flour contains, the more elastic is a dough made with it. Unfortunately all-purpose flour does not suit our needs. It's a mixture of various wheats whose gluten content is too low to yield really good bread. The kind of flour you will want to procure is the sort that is milled specifically for bread making —that is, bread flour.

Bread flour is high in gluten and will aid you in baking perfect sourdough loaves. Since it is not readily available from the shelves of your local supermarket, you are going to have to do some hunting to obtain it. There are basically three ways for you to get the kind of high gluten flour with which you will want to bake all your sourdough bread.

If you're an absolute incorrigible sourdough-nut, the first way of getting the flour you want is in 100-pound sacks from a commercial food broker. You can find him listed in the phone book. You will have to go to his warehouse to pick up the flour, but the price per pound will most likely be lower than supermarket flour prices. Since food brokers are inclined to deal in specifics, tell him you want a high gluten, patent flour suitable for bread making. If you find him incredulous, say that a flour with a protein content of 13 to 14 per cent will fill your needs perfectly. That will answer any questions he could possibly have. P.S. . . take a friend with you to the warehouse. Unless you're a longshoreman, 100-pound flour sacks are back-breakers.

The second and most practical means of obtaining a high gluten flour is directly from a small, local bakery. The bakeries found in supermarkets, for example, have the kind of flour you want. Bakers are usually great people and you will find them most willing to help you.

They'll be happy to sell you 5 or 10 pounds of good bread flour at a reasonable price. Most folks find this easier than lugging 100-pound sacks.

The last option for obtaining bread flour is from a health foods or gourmet store. You might run into a problem, though, because these stores offer a sometimes confusing array of various flours. The selection is often huge. Since the labeling of these sundry flours is perplexing, ask someone in the store to help you. Look for "hard wheat" or "winter wheat" flour. These are both essentially the same and are good bread flours with a high gluten content. If you buy a flour that is labeled specifically as "high gluten," follow the directions as given on the package. Usually this kind of flour must be mixed with all-purpose flour because its gluten content is higher than that found in a bread flour. In this case, you might have to do some experimenting to get the results you want.

Bread Batter

As with the baked goods in Sundry Sourdough Sustenance, all the breads found in this section are based on an aged batter made of flour, starter, and water to which additional ingredients are later added to complete the recipe. Bread Batter is allowed to mature between 72° and 77° for 24 hours before being used. Although Ambrosia Batter and Bread Batter are similar, the amount of starter added to each is different because their eventual uses are different. With Ambrosia Batter, an entire cup of starter is added to 1½ cups of flour and one cup of water. With Bread Batter the same amounts of flour and water are used, but only 1 tablespoon of starter is set to work to begin the fermentation of the mixture.

A larger amount of starter is added to Ambrosia Batter to insure plenty of sourdough tang. Remember that Ambrosia Batter is usually given an extra boost with the help of a chemical leavener such as baking powder or soda. While these aid in making biscuits and griddlecakes light, they do tend to lessen the flavor of the sourdough. With Bread Batter it isn't so much the amount of sourdough flavor we're interested in as the vigorous growth of the wild yeast. Since true sourdough bread rises over a long period of time and contains no commercial yeast or chemical leaveners, the flavor of the sourdough comes through naturally. Most importantly, however, THE WILD YEAST MUST BE IN A VERY ACTIVE STATE IF IT IS TO RAISE BREAD PROPERLY. This is the key to successful sourdough baking. By beginning a bread batter with only 1 tablespoon of good fresh starter, the wild yeast is allowed to grow at its own lazy pace. At the end of the 24-hour growing period, it has reached its maximum growth and is then in ideal condition for use in bread. Although a well-ripened Ambrosia Batter has fine sourdough flavor, the wild yeast cells in it have lost some of their vitality and lack the leavening power to raise a stiff bread dough. Ambrosia Batter is great for making griddlecakes and the like but not good for making bread.

To insure that Bread Batter is full of wild yeast cells which are in the peak of condition, follow these two rules:

First, USE ONLY A FRESH, ACTIVE STARTER. If your starter has not been used in the last two days, sweeten the pot and allow it to re-ferment for 24 hours before using (see the instructions on page 26). This will insure that the Bread Batter will receive a dose of wild yeast that's in fine fettle. A half-dead starter does not provide a Bread Batter with enough live wild yeast cells to have it ripen properly. This is one of the principal reasons most people have trouble baking true sourdough bread at home, and why invariably all sourdough recipes found in conventional cookbooks require the use of commercial yeast along with the wild yeast. Needless to say, the use of commercial yeast materially detracts from a true sourdough flavor. All the bread recipes in this book use wild yeast as the sole leavener, thus insuring bread of extraordinarily fine flavor.

Second, AGE THE BREAD BATTER BETWEEN 72° AND 77° FOR EXACTLY 24 HOURS. Carefully controlling the temperature at which the Bread Batter is allowed to ferment and then aging it for exactly 24 hours aids in catching it for use when the wild yeast has reached its maximum growth. If the temperature is too low, the wild yeast will not grow properly. If the temperature is too high, the yeast might overgrow and start to lose its vitality before you use it. If a Bread Batter is used before the 24-hour time cycle is completed, the wild yeast will not have been given sufficient time to complete its fermentation. The resulting bread will probably rise well but will lack sourdough flavor. On the other hand, if you were to use a Bread Batter 3 or 4 hours after the normal 24-hour time cycle has been completed, some of the wild yeast would have begun to die and the Bread Batter would most likely be over-fermented.

94

As you can see, aging a Bread Batter correctly is crucial to the making of properly risen sourdough bread. Although the procedure for maturing a Bread Batter is more exacting, it is not really too much more difficult than for Ambrosia Batter. Both require a 24-hour time cycle and must be kept quite warm. With Ambrosia Batter you can cheat a little with regard to how long the batter is aged and at what temperature it's kept. For example, an Ambrosia Batter maintained 20 hours at 70° will still make great griddlecakes, but a Bread Batter kept under those conditions will not produce sour bread of good flavor. The aging of a Bread Batter cannot be compromised; it must be done correctly.

Finding an area in your house that's between 72° and 77° might prove to be troublesome, so here are a few suggestions as to where you might look. Be sure to use a thermometer to determine the correct temperature of each area you test. A gas oven with a pilot light usually makes a perfect sourdough incubating area. A closet with a strong light bulb is sometimes warm enough to do the job. Try your attic. Most of the time it's warmer than the downstairs rooms you pay so much to heat. If you can't find a suitable area, rig up a cardboard box with a small (7½-watt) light. By cutting holes in it you can easily regulate the warmth inside the box.

The recipe for Bread Batter is:

1 cup warm water
1½ cups bread flour

1 Tablespoon FRESH, ACTIVE starter.
See page 26 for "Sweetening the Pot."

Combine and mix the ingredients in a 2-quart bowl. Bread Batter is thicker than Ambrosia Batter when first mixed. Cover and set aside in an area of 72° to 77° warmth for exactly 24 hours. Bear in mind that the aging procedure for Bread Batter must be followed carefully. At the end of maturation, Bread Batter should be very bubbly and frothy. This is your guarantee of bread that will rise properly and will be delicious with sourdough flavor. If the Bread Batter is not active, it will not produce good bread.

Replenish the starter by discarding all but one tablespoon and mixing in 2 cups of flour and 1½ cups of warm water.

Kneading

In biscuit making, kneading the dough is done primarily to aid in mixing the ingredients. With the making of bread, not only are the ingredients mixed but the gluten (bread protein) in the dough is also developed by the kneading process. This makes the dough stretchy and elastic so that it can catch and hole the CO_2 given off by the wild yeast, thus causing the bread to rise. Complete development of gluten is critical to successful bread making. Developing a sourdough bread dough usually requires from 300 to 400 strokes, and depending upon one's speed, this could take from 15 to 30 minutes working time.

Don't look with disdain upon the effort and time involved in properly developing a bread dough. Wielding a dough with your own two good hands will produce a far better bread than any home mixer. Mechanical devices simply cannot duplicate the motion of the human hand. Besides, kneading is therapeutic. Turning a dough onto a bread board and kneading it until it's smooth and elastic helps to ease the stresses and strains of our lives and move them into the background. It's a great way to forget problems and better exercise than can be gotten at the health spa. And if you get tired you can always take a coffee break in the middle of the kneading process. It won't hurt the dough at all. Just cover it with a damp cloth so that it won't dry out, and take as long a break as you wish.

All cookbooks dealing with baked goods offer a word or two about the science of kneading. Most go into elaborate detail as to exactly how the dough should be shaped, shoved, pushed, pulled, twisted, and turned. Such instructions are for the most part unnecessary. To develop gluten satisfactorily, the only thing a bread dough requires is an energetic workout. Some instructions on kneading have been included here, but as you gain experience you will learn the methods which work best for you.

In general, kneading goes something like this: First, combine the bread batter with the rest of the ingredients in the order as given in the recipe. Mix until the dough can no longer be stirred by hand. Turn the dough and all the still unmixed ingredients onto a kneading surface. This should be an area of at least 18 x 18 inches which is smooth and clean. Surfaces of formica (counter tops) or hardwood are good. Soft wood bread boards made of such materials as pine and fir are poor. They can transfer off flavors to the dough and splinter easily.

From the point when the dough is turned onto the kneading surface, it should be handled with authority. Gather the dough pieces and, as much as possible, shape them into a ball. With the palm of the hand push it down. Then fold the outer edge of the flattened dough towards you so that it forms a mound. Folding the dough increases its height so it can again be kneaded by pushing it down with the heel of the hand. Each time the dough is kneaded, it should be shifted a quarter turn. This helps to insure that all the dough is kneaded the same amount. During the process of pushing, folding, and shifting the dough, allow it to absorb the loose flour and other ingredients on the bread board.

As the working of the dough proceeds, you may find it necessary to add additional small amounts of flour to keep it from sticking. Because flour types vary a good deal, it's impossible to specify in a recipe the exact amount of flour needed to avoid sticking and insure proper dough stiffness. Practice in bread making will make you the best judge of this. As the kneading continues and the gluten develops, less and less additional flour will be required until finally you will be able to work the dough on a completely unfloured bread board. During the kneading process avoid adding too much flour because dough can be made stiff to the degree that wild yeast cannot raise it properly.

After several minutes of kneading, the dough will begin to exhibit definite signs of becoming elastic and smooth. When this starts to occur, it will not be necessary to refold the dough with each knead. At this point you can knead using both hands in a criss-cross motion. It's less tiring than using just one hand, and helps to speed up the whole process. Try this: With each downward stroke of the hand, dig your fingers firmly into the dough as you push it away. The more you pull and stretch the dough the better it is. When the stroke is finished, roll the dough back towards you to position it for the next knead with the other hand. This will take some getting used to but dough can be kneaded very quickly with this method. You'll also find that it gives you a whale of a workout, but what the heck, it's good exercise.

If you don't care for the criss-cross method of massaging a dough, you can easily evolve your own technique. Almost any forceful manipulation helps to develop a dough, but always be firm of hand and don't baby it. Remember, it generally takes from 300 to 400 firm strokes to make a dough adequately supple and elastic.

As a dough reaches its proper stage of gluten development, it becomes smooth and satiny. It will feel like soft putty and will have a slight stickiness to it. Professional bakers describe a well-kneaded dough as feeling very much like the skin on the inside of the forearm. There is accuracy to that description. To check for gluten development, let the dough rest for a few minutes while you take a rest. Then pinch a small portion of it and pull away slowly. If the dough stretches about one inch without breaking, the kneading is finished. If it tends to break easily, you had best knead it for a few more minutes.

There is another way to test for gluten. Take a small piece of dough which has been allowed **99** to rest for a few minutes and stretch it using both hands. If it can be spread to a relatively thin film without breaking, the gluten has been properly developed.

With a little practice, you will be able to readily tell when a dough has been kneaded sufficiently.

Once a dough has been kneaded, it should be shaped for baking by flattening it slightly and then folding the outer edges together, pinching them to make a seam. This gives the dough an even finish. If you don't shape the dough to your liking on the first try, it can be handled and reshaped with no ill effect. What you are trying to achieve is a dough with a smooth skin and all seams tightly sealed. When you have shaped the dough the way you want it, place the loaf —seams down—in a bread pan or on a cookie sheet.

Raising the Dough

After dough has been kneaded and shaped, it rises. This is the period during which the bread is "blown up" like a balloon by the wild yeast. It usually takes sourdough bread about twice as long to rise as does ordinary bread made with commercial yeast. Depending on the condition of the wild yeast in the bread batter and the stiffness of the dough, a loaf of sourdough bread will take anywhere from 3 to 6 hours to rise to its full height. The more aged the bread batter and the stiffer the dough, the longer the bread will take to rise. Don't be impatient, it takes wild yeast considerable time to impart its marvelous flavor.

All the bread recipes in this book require that the dough rise only once. If you want a sourer loaf, it's a good practice to let the dough rise once before shaping it for the final rising. This additional time lets the wild yeast work longer to give the bread more flavor. To let a dough rise once (or even twice), place it in a lightly-greased bowl and cover tightly. Place the dough in a warm place to rise for about 2 hours. Let the dough double in bulk. To test a risen dough for doubled bulk, punch two fingers into it about a half-inch. If the impression left by the two fingers remains, the wild yeast has finished its work. If the dough has a tendency to bounce back, give it more time to rise. Once the dough has risen once or twice for additional sourness, knead it lightly and briefly (30 seconds) and shape it for its final rising.

Allow loaves which have been shaped and are being raised for the final time plenty of warmth (between 75° and 110°). The best place to let it rise prior to baking is right in the oven. Before putting the loaf in, preheat the oven on its lowest setting of "warm." Once an oven has been prewarmed, it will retain enough warmth over a period of several hours to raise a dough to its full height.

The most critical factor in the raising of sourdough bread is the prevention of a crust forming on the skin of the dough. This can present a problem due to the prolonged time period a good sourdough loaf requires to rise satisfactorily. The crust forms a barrier against which the wild yeast cannot leaven the bread. To prevent crusting, two simple precautions are advised.

First, brush the loaf with melted butter, margarine, or shortening before letting it rise. This aids in sealing in moisture. Don't use oil, though; it does not provide a protective coating.

Second, let the loaf rise in a humid atmosphere. Do this by placing a pan of boiling water on the bottom of the oven every hour or so. Air of high humidity will prevent the loaf from drying out. The boiling water also helps in keeping the oven warm.

Bread should be raised until it has fully doubled in bulk. Since sourdough bread rises very little as it is being baked, it's important to let it rise as much as possible prior to baking. A loaf that has risen fully will have a voluminous, ballooned appearance. At the first signs of the dough falling or the skin beginning to break, the bread should be immediately baked. After the second hour of raising, it's a good idea to check the dough occasionally so that it can be baked as soon as the loaf has reached its maximum expansion. Most novices to bread making make the common error of baking the bread too soon. A loaf which has been allowed to rise in its entirety will appear to have doubled its original bulk and then some.

Crusts

There are many different types of crusts that can be put on bread. Here are a few suggestions:

Soft Crust: Brush the loaf with melted butter 20 minutes after the baking has started and again when the loaf is taken from the oven. Cover with a cloth as the loaf is cooling.

Medium Hard Crust: Follow the normal instructions for raising sourdough bread and allow the loaf to cool uncovered after being baked.

Medium Hard, Shiny Crust: Brush the loaf with a mixture of one egg white mixed with 1 tablespoon of cold water prior to baking and again after the loaf has baked 20 minutes. Allow the loaf to cool uncovered.

Hard Crust: Before starting to raise the dough, brush it with water instead of melted butter. After the loaf has risen, use a clean spray bottle filled with cold water and spray it prior to baking. Spray the loaf again after it has baked 10 minutes. Allow the loaf to cool uncovered. Since a loaf baked with a hard crust is not coated with butter, extra care must be taken to insure that it doesn't crust while being raised. Keep the air inside the oven humid by replacing the boiling water in the bottom of the oven as often as needed.

Hardest and Shiniest Crust: This produces a hard, shiny and crunchy crust. Instead of brushing the loaf with melted butter before raising it, use a mixture of 1 cup water mixed with 1 teaspoon salt. Using a clean spray bottle, spray the loaf with the salted water just prior to baking. At 5-minute intervals, spray the loaf for the first 15 minutes it is being baked. Allow the finished loaf to cool uncovered. If the loaf has been sprayed with a sufficient amount of water, the crust will be quite shiny.

Baking

By all means avail yourself of a good oven thermometer to test the accuracy of your oven's thermostat. Baking loaves in an oven set for 400° but actually roasting them at 450° will certainly not be of help in your pursuit of fine quality sourdough bread. It's not unusual for an oven thermostat to be off 50° or more, and taking the time to check for this is highly recommended. Oven thermometers are inexpensive and fully worth the invaluable service they render.

Although bread is raised in the oven, it's not necessary to remove it to pre-heat the oven for baking. Just make sure the oven is set for "bake" (not preheat) and turn the thermostat to the desired setting. The period during which the oven heats up will provide the unbaked loaf additional rising time before it is set by the heat.

Prospector's Bread

In the days of the Gold Rush there were as many "Prospector's Breads" as there were prospectors. No set recipes existed because a gold digger would use whatever ingredients he happened to have on hand, knowing full well that if he made his bread with sourdough, it would be good. The recipe listed below makes bread which is close to the kind that helped provide many a miner with a hearty meal. It does, however, lack one ingredient which numerous prospectors found frequent occasion to use—bone butter.

104

Often finding themselves without cow butter, prospectors would use a trick invented by the buffalo hunters of the Old West. Here's what an old sourdough by the name of Henry Davis wrote about bone butter in his diary on the 8th of January, 1888:

We ran out of butter, so Smith said to bring in a big set of caribou horns. I chopped the horns in two pieces and he said to cut that up into pieces ten inches long. He then gave me the big pot and said to put the horns in it and that he would show me how to make butter. I filled the pot and he added water (melted snow) and we boiled this for two nights and a day, then took it off the stove, took out the bones and placed it on the floor to cool. In about two hours, I looked at it and there were about two inches of white butter on top of the water. He took off the butter and put more salt in it and had as good a butter as any except that it was white in color. I was glad to learn how to make butter, for I won't have to go without it.*

Although bone butter is not available, you can substitute bacon fat or salt pork lard, both of which were common ingredients for Prospector's Bread during the days of the Gold Rush.

1 recipe altered Bread Batter
    Use 1 cup warm water, 1 cup bread flour, ½ cup cracked wheat, and 1 tablespoon fresh starter. Follow the normal Bread Batter aging directions as given on page 94.
1½ to 2 cups bread flour
¼ cup salt pork lard or bacon   1 Tablespoon sugar
  fat, melted   1 teaspoon salt

Mix the Bread Batter with 1¼ cups of flour, the lard, sugar, and salt. Stir until the dough pulls away from the sides of the mixing bowl. Turn this soft dough and the unmixed ingredients onto a kneading surface sprinkled with ¼ cup of flour. Knead with vigor,

105

*From *Sourdough Sagas*, edited by Dr. Herbert Heller. New York: Ballantine Books, 1972.

allowing the dough to absorb the flour and unmixed ingredients. Sparingly add additional flour as required to prevent sticking. Knead until the dough is smooth and elastic. Shape into a round loaf. Placing the seams downward, put the loaf on a cookie sheet which has been sprinkled with cornmeal. Brush with melted lard. Put into a warm oven in which a pan of boiling water has been placed. Keep the oven off while the dough is rising and replace the boiling water as necessary to prevent the dough from crusting. When the loaf has doubled in bulk, bake at 400° for 45 to 50 minutes or until the crust is nicely browned. Cool the baked loaf on a wire rack.

Old-Fashioned White Bread

This recipe makes a wonderful, old-fashioned white bread. Some of the old bread recipes of this type required that bread be made only with a starter in which milk was used instead of water. This has been simplified (and the recipe improved upon) by adding powdered milk at the time the bread is mixed.

1 recipe Bread Batter. See page 95
1½ to 2 cups bread flour
⅓ cup powdered milk
¼ cup butter, melted

3 Tablespoons sugar
1½ teaspoons salt

Mix the Bread Batter with 1¼ cups flour, the powdered milk, butter, sugar, and salt. Stir until the dough pulls away from the sides of the bowl, and then turn this soft dough and any unmixed ingredients onto a kneading surface sprinkled with ¼ cup of bread flour. Knead the dough well, allowing it to absorb the flour and unmixed ingredients. Sparingly add additional flour as required to prevent sticking. Knead until the dough is smooth and elastic. Shape the loaf and put it into a buttered bread pan of appropriate size, placing seams in the dough downward. Brush with melted butter and put in a warm oven into which a pan of boiling water has been placed. Turn the oven off. Allow the dough to rise. Bake at 375° for 45 minutes or until the bread shrinks away from the sides of the pan and sounds hollow when tapped. When the baking is completed, remove the loaf from its pan and cool on a wire rack. Leaving a baked loaf in its pan to cool will cause it to become soggy because the loaf sweats as it gives off heat.

Graham Bread

A hellfire and brimstone Presbyterian minister by the name of Sylvester Graham swept America with his health food ideas in the middle 1800s. The irascible Graham denounced white flour (it had no substance), meat (it promoted sexual sin), soups (they provided no opportunity for chewing) and, naturally, alcohol (a generally debilitating substance). He felt the "Yankee race" was headed for certain doom. Surprisingly, Grahamism came to be embraced by such notables as Horace Greeley and Thomas Edison, but apparently his system didn't entirely agree with him because Dr. Graham died when he was barely 57, in 1856.

For all his eccentricity, Graham was absolutely right about the worth of unbolted (whole wheat) flour. For flavor and nutritional value whole grain flour is superior to the bleached variety which is in such common usage today. The recipe below is for a whole wheat bread which calls for Graham flour. If you can't get it, substitute stone ground whole wheat flour; it's almost identical to Graham's invention. Since Graham and whole wheat flours are rich in wheat germ oil, both should be stored in the refrigerator to preserve their freshness.

You will notice that this recipe calls for no shortening; fats of all kinds were prohibited under the Graham system. Don't let that bother you, though, because this bread is equally as good without it . . . just chewy like French bread. If you don't care for chewy bread, add ¼ cup of melted butter to the recipe. That'll fix it.

1 recipe altered Bread Batter
    Use 2 cups Graham flour, 1 cup warm water, ⅓ cup honey and 1 tablespoon active
    starter. Follow the normal instructions for aging a Bread Batter as given on page 94.
1½ - 2 cups Graham flour   ¼ cup powdered milk
                            1 teaspoon salt

108

The powdered milk isn't a usual ingredient in Graham Bread but does materially improve its flavor. You can leave it out if you're a stalwart Grahamite.

Combine the Bread Batter, 1½ cups of the flour, powdered milk, and salt. (Also add the melted butter at this time, if desired.) Stir until the dough pulls away from the sides of the mixing bowl. Turn onto a kneading surface floured lightly with Graham flour. Knead until the dough smooths somewhat. Add more flour as required to prevent the dough from sticking. Because this is a whole wheat bread, it will not be so smooth as one containing all bread flour. Form the dough into a round loaf, brush with melted butter and place it in a lightly greased pie tin. Let rise in an oven which has been preheated on its lowest setting of warm. Turn the oven off. Place a pan of boiling water on the floor of the oven to keep the air moist and prevent the dough from crusting. Since whole wheat bread does not rise as high as bread made wholly with bread flour, bake the loaf as soon as it approaches a doubled bulk. Bake at 375° for 50 minutes. Allow the loaf to cool on a wire rack.

Graham recommended that his bread be eaten plain and then only when it was a day or two old to prevent it from gluing one's innards. Nevertheless, you will find Graham bread to be the tastiest when it is fresh from the oven and smothered with butter.

Peasant Black Bread

This is the heavy, black bread which fed Europe's peasantry during the 1,000 years of the Dark Ages. It is rich in flavor and perfect for those redolent deli sandwiches thick with

Monterey Jack cheese, corned beef or pastrami, and dripping with a generous spread of eye-watering hot mustard. Any sandwich made thus should naturally be washed down with nothing less than huge quantities of cold beer.

For this recipe you will need ½ cup of fine bread crumbs toasted to a deep brown. This helps to give the loaf a dark color. Toast the crumbs in an oven set at 250°, turning them frequently so they bake evenly.

1 recipe altered Bread Batter
> Use 1½ cups rye flour, 1 cup warm water, and 1 tablespoon active starter. Follow the normal instructions for aging a Bread Batter as given on page 94.

1½ cups bread flour	2 Tablespoons dark molasses
½ cup toasted, fine bread crumbs	1 teaspoon salt
2 Tablespoons butter, melted	

Mix the Bread Batter with the ½ cup of bread crumbs, 1 cup of the bread flour, the melted butter, dark molasses, and salt. Stir until the dough pulls away from the sides of the mixing bowl and then turn the soft dough and any unmixed ingredients onto a kneading surface that has been floured with the remaining ½ cup of bread flour. Knead the dough well, allowing it to absorb the flour on the kneading surface. Sparingly add additional flour as required to prevent the dough from sticking and to bring it to proper stiffness. Knead the dough until it is smooth and elastic. Owing to the presence of the rye flour and bread crumbs, the dough will not be so smooth and elastic as one made with all bread flour. Shape the loaf so that it is round, and place it on a cookie sheet (seams downward) which has been sprinkled liberally with white or yellow cornmeal. Brush the loaf with melted butter and place it in an oven which has been preheated on its lowest setting of warm. Turn the oven off. Place a pan of boiling water in the oven to prevent the rising loaf from crusting. Black bread does not rise as high as does other sourdough bread, so when it starts to approach anything close to doubling its original bulk, it should be baked. Bake at 400° for 50 minutes. Allow to cool on a wire rack when the baking has been completed.

Sourcream Herb Bread

Here is a unique dinner bread, perfect for a special occasion.

1 recipe Bread Batter—See page 95.
2¾ to 3 cups bread flour   ½ Tablespoon sugar
½ cup sour cream, warmed   1 teaspoon salt

Combine and mix the Bread Batter, 2¾ cups bread flour, sour cream, sugar, and salt. Stir until the dough pulls away from the sides of the mixing bowl and then turn this dough and any unmixed ingredients onto a kneading surface lightly sprinkled with bread flour.

Knead the dough, allowing it to absorb the flour and other ingredients. Add additional flour sparingly to prevent the dough from sticking as the kneading continues. Knead the dough until the gluten is well developed. This dough will be quite stiff. Set the dough aside after covering it with a damp towel.

Next prepare the herb seasoning:

2 Tablespoons instant minced onion (dehydrated)
2 Tablespoons Parmesan cheese
1 teaspoon bell pepper flakes (dehydrated)
½ teaspoon salt

¼ teaspoon pepper
¼ teaspoon sweet basil
¼ teaspoon oregano

Combine all the above ingredients and mix. Roll out the dough to a thickness of ¼- to ½-inch. Sprinkle the seasonings evenly over the rolled dough. Using your hand, gently press the seasonings into the dough. Roll up the dough as tightly as possible in jellyroll fashion. Shape the loaf and pinch all the seams shut. All seams should be at the bottom of the loaf. Put the loaf on a cookie sheet sprinkled with cornmeal. Place it in an oven which has been preheated on its lowest setting of warm. Brush with melted butter. Turn off the oven. Place a pan of boiling water in the bottom of the oven and replace as often as necessary to insure the inside air stays moist. Bake at 375° for 45 to 50 minutes. Cool the loaf on a wire rack.

San Francisco Sourdough French Bread

Of all sourdough breads, the kind that comes from San Francisco is the most famous, has the fewest ingredients and is, ironically, the most difficult to bake. It would be only fair to point out that you can expect the bread which you bake at home to vary slightly from the San Francisco loaves. But don't be dismayed. Even in San Francisco itself, bread made by different bakeries is very perceivably different. Various wild yeast types, equipment, and weather all serve to alter the character of sourdough French bread. With practice you will be able to bake crusty, crunchy loaves, sapid with the fragrant scent of sourdough which your family and friends will rave about.

Following are two recipes, the first of which is easier than the second. Start with the first and then progress to the second if you feel so inclined. Recipe II is more difficult, but it does produce a loaf which is closer to the genuine article though, frankly, it is a lot of work.

Both recipes call for the same ingredients; it's the way the dough is handled and the method of baking that distinguishes the two. Don't be surprised at the amazingly small number of ingredients required to make sourdough French bread. These are exactly the same ingredients that are used by the bakers in San Francisco . . . flour, water, salt, and nothing more.

Recipe I

1 recipe Bread Batter—See page 95.
2 to 2¼ cups bread flour   1 teaspoon salt

Mix the Bread Batter with 2 cups of flour and the salt. Stir until the dough pulls away from the sides of the mixing bowl. Turn the dough and all the unmixed ingredients onto a kneading surface sprinkled lightly with bread flour. Knead the dough, allowing it to absorb the flour and unmixed dough. Add more flour as is necessary to keep the dough from sticking. It is important that sourdough French bread be kneaded very thoroughly so that the gluten in the dough is developed completely. Test the dough for gluten as described on page 99. If need be, count your strokes; 400 are usually sufficient to properly develop gluten. After the kneading is done, allow the dough to rest a few minutes before shaping it into the customary French long loaf. Shape the dough and place the seams downward; put it on a cookie sheet sprinkled with white or yellow corn-meal. Brush the dough with cold water. Place the dough in an oven which has been preheated at its lowest setting of "warm" and in which a pan of boiling water has been placed. Turn the oven off. Change the pan of boiling water as often as is necessary to keep the air inside the oven warm and moist. When the dough starts to show signs of having risen well, using a **new** razor blade gently make three ¼-inch deep diagonal slash marks across the loaf. Once the bread has fully doubled in bulk, carefully brush or spray the loaf with cold water. Place a fresh pan of briskly boiling water in the bottom of the oven. Turn the oven to 400°. Brush or spray the loaf again after it has baked for 15

114

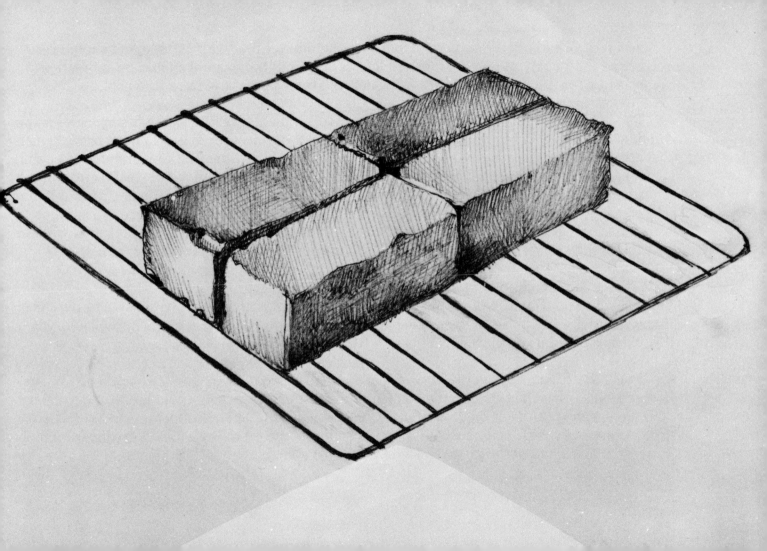

minutes. A loaf usually requires from 45 to 50 minutes total baking time and should be baked thoroughly. When the finished loaf comes from the oven, it should be sprayed or brushed for the final time with cold water and then set on a wire rack to cool.

The second recipe for sourdough French bread is much the same as the first except for the method of baking. What we are going to attempt is a duplication of the famous brick hearth ovens of San Francisco, and this takes some ingenuity. During the first few minutes of baking San Francisco sourdough, the bread is thoroughly inundated with billows of steam. Further, the sourdough baker does not use pans of any kind in the baking of his bread. He peels (places) the risen loaves directly onto the hot brick floor of the oven. Along with the steam, this helps to raise the loaf all the more. The steam also aids in developing the crust which is so unique to French bread.

Since it is unlikely that you want to equip your oven with steam jets and a brick hearth, here's what you can do to improvise. Go to a building materials supply house and purchase four fire bricks. Lay these on top of the oven rack in two rows of two across. This will give you a baking surface of 8 x 16 inches.

To get the risen loaf onto the hot brick at the time of baking, you have two options. The first is the easiest. Raise the bread on a section of aluminum foil backed by a piece of cardboard and then simply slide it onto the hot brick, foil and all. The second method is the more traditional and a good deal more difficult. Raise the bread on a piece of stiff cardboard which has been very generously sprinkled with cornmeal. When the loaf has risen, peel it directly onto the hot brick by jerking the cardboard out from underneath. It's a neat trick which requires practice. Once the risen loaf touches the hot brick, it cannot be moved until after the first 15 minutes of baking are completed.

Improvising for the steam jets is harder than creating the baking surface. Two things will help. First, make sure at the time the loaf is baked that the pan of water placed in the bottom of the oven is boiling very rapidly. Secondly, for the first 15 minutes the loaf is baked, at 5-minute intervals, spray it with cold water. These two things will greatly aid in affecting a finished loaf with a fine, crunchy crust.

Recipe II

Follow Recipe I up to the point where the dough has been sufficiently kneaded and is to be placed on the cookie sheet. Instead of placing the loaf on the cookie sheet, place it either on a section of aluminum foil which has been sprinkled with cornmeal or directly onto a piece of stiff, thin cardboard which has been sprinkled generously with cornmeal. If you have decided to use the foil technique, use a piece of stiff cardboard as a backing. Brush the dough with cold water. Put the loaf in an oven which has been preheated on the lowest setting of "warm." Turn the oven off. The loaf can be placed directly atop the fire brick which has been previously installed. Place a pan of boiling water on the bottom of the oven. As with Recipe I, replace the boiling water as needed to keep the oven warm and to prevent the dough from crusting. When the dough starts to show signs of rising, using a new razor blade, gently make three ¼-inch deep diagonal slash marks across the loaf. When the dough has fully doubled in bulk, with great care remove it from the oven. Turn the oven to "preheat" (so that it heats from **both** the top and the bottom) and heat it at the highest thermostat setting for 45 minutes to heat the bricks. After the 45-minute heating period for the bricks is completed, turn the thermostat to 400°, turn the oven dial to bake, and open the oven door. At this point pull the rack out with the bricks on it and (depending on your method) slide or jerk the loaf onto the hot bricks. Give the loaf a light spray of the cold water. Leave the oven door open. The bricks will be hot enough to start the baking process from the bottom of the loaf. When the indicator light flashes on showing the oven has cooled to 400° (this will take from 3 to 4 minutes), spray the loaf again and gently slide the rack into the oven. Recheck to make sure the dial has been turned from preheat to bake. For the first 15 minutes of baking, at 5-minute intervals, spray cold water on the loaf. The entire baking process should take from 45 to 50 minutes. Sourdough French bread should be thoroughly baked. When the loaf comes from the oven, it should be sprayed for the final time with cold water and then set on a wire rack to cool.

Seattle Sourdough Bread

Although it's not quite as famous as its San Francisco relative, Seattle Sourdough Bread is easily as good. Make this bread and see why Jake O'Shaughnessey's will use none other as its house bread.

1 recipe altered Bread Batter
> Use 1½ cups bread flour, 1 cup warm water, 2 tablespoons cracked wheat, and 1 tablespoon of active starter. Follow the normal instructions for aging a Bread Batter as given on page 94.

2½ to 3 cups bread flour.   1 teaspoon salt

½ cup real sour cream

Mix the Bread Batter with 2½ cups of flour, the sour cream, and salt. Stir until the dough pulls away from the sides of the mixing bowl. Turn the dough and all the unmixed ingredients onto a kneading surface sprinkled with bread flour. Knead the dough allowing it to absorb the flour. Add more flour as is necessary to keep the dough from sticking. Knead the dough very thoroughly (from 300 to 400 strokes). Once the kneading is completed, cover the dough and let it rise in a warm area for two to three hours or until doubled in bulk. An oven preheated on a setting of warm and then turned off is ideal as a dough raising area. Once the dough has risen, punch it down, knead it lightly, and form it into a round loaf. Place the loaf on a cookie sheet (seams downward) that has been sprinkled with corn meal. Brush the loaf with whole egg that has been beaten with a teaspoon of water and a pinch of salt. Place the loaf in the preheated warm oven and put a pan of boiling water on the bottom. Change the water as often as necessary to insure moist warm air for the rising of the dough. Do **not** slash the loaf with a razor blade. Once the loaf has risen, brush it very gently with the egg mixture and turn the oven to 400°. Bake for 50 minutes or until it is a deep golden brown. Cool on a wire rack.

TROUBLESHOOTING

This section will help pinpoint difficulties you might have in executing recipes. Most persons first learning the technique of wild yeast cookery run into a little trouble. Fermentation of any kind, after all, can be tricky and in the end, practice is really by far the best guide. The most important factors in the preparation of sourdough are making sure your starter is in good shape and properly aging the Ambrosia and Bread Batters. Throughout this section you will see references to sweetening the pot and correct fermentation procedures. These are the secrets of successful sourdough cooking.

GRIDDLECAKES

Problem	Solutions
Cakes are heavy.	1. The starter was old. See page 26 for sweetening the pot.
	2. Assuming the starter was in good condition, the fermentation of the Ambrosia Batter was not done correctly. See page 33.
	3. If the starter was in good condition and the Ambrosia Batter properly fermented, try re-fermenting the griddlecake batter itself. Time permitting, place the griddlecake batter in a warm place for two or three hours. It will become light and frothy.
	4. Add ¼ teaspoon baking soda.

121

Cakes are sticking to pan.	1. See instructions on page 38 for "seasoning" a pan or add 1/8-inch cooking oil to the bottom of the pan and turn the heat to high. When the oil smokes, pour off the excess and allow the pan to cool slightly before grilling.
Cakes are not sour.	1. Make sure the starter is in good condition, and carefully follow the Ambrosia Batter aging instructions starting on page 33.
	2. Leave out the baking soda as called for in the recipe. This will make the cakes heavier but more sour.
	3. Make the starter as given in Method II on page 24.
Cakes are too sour.	Add ¼ to ½ teaspoon baking soda.

BISCUITS

Problem	Solutions
Biscuits are heavy.	1. The starter was old. See page 26 for sweetening the pot.
	2. If the starter was in good condition then the Ambrosia Batter may not have been aged correctly. See page 33.
	3. Assuming fresh starter, an active and properly fermented Ambrosia Batter, the biscuits were not allowed to rise long enough in warm temperature. Raise biscuits two hours in an area of at least 75°.

122

| Biscuits not tender. | 1. Properly cut in the shortening. See page 66 or the Glossary. |
| | 2. Do not over knead. Use 15 to 20 strokes at the most. |

Biscuits not sour.	1. The starter was old. See page 26 for sweetening the pot.
	2. If the starter was in good condition, then the Ambrosia Batter was not aged in an area that was warm enough. Or, it was not aged long enough. See instructions beginning on page 33.
	3. Try making a starter by Method II as described on page 24.

| Finished biscuits are doughy | Reduce heat and bake longer. |

SOURDOUGH BREAD

Problem   **Solutions**

Heavy bread	1. The starter was not in good condition. See page 26 for sweetening the pot.
	2. Assuming the starter was in good condition, the Bread Batter was not fermented properly. See page 94.
	3. Allow more time for the bread to rise. Also make sure that the rising loaf does not "crust." Read the instructions beginning on page 100.
	4. Too much flour was added to the Bread Batter, making the dough too stiff. If this is the difficulty, reduce the amount of flour added to the Bread Batter.

Bread skin splits before bread has risen properly	1. Not enough kneading. See instructions beginning on page 96. 2. Wrong flour used. See page 90.
Not enough sour	1. The starter was in poor condition. See pages 26–27. 2. Assuming the starter was in good condition, the Bread Batter was not aged properly. See page 94. 3. Try allowing the bread dough to rise once before shaping it into a loaf. See page 101. 4. Keep in mind the addition of baking power, soda or commercial yeast to a bread recipe will definitely lessen the sourness of the finished bread. 5. Make the starter by Method II as described on page 24. It's terrific.
Bread crust is pale.	Increase the oven heat.
Bread baked on a cookie sheet flattens out	Add a little more flour to stiffen the dough.

GLOSSARY

This section has been provided for the cook who finds the vast mélange of cooking jargon confusing. Such words as "cut in," "fold," "rest" and so on can befuddle even old hands at the art of cooking. This list should greatly help you tread your way through the sometimes seemingly tortuous recipes found in this book and others.

All purpose flour is a mixture of hard and soft wheats suitable for cakes, pies, griddlecakes and biscuits. It is not suitable for the production of good, well-raised bread. All-purpose flour is low in gluten.

Ambrosia Batter is a mixture of 1 cup starter, 1½ cups all purpose flour and 1 cup warm water. It is aged for 24 hours at 75° to develop a tangy sourdough flavor. Ambrosia Batter or variations of it are the basis for most of the recipes found in Sundry Sourdough Sustenance.

Bake means to cook in an oven with dry heat.

Beat means to mix ingredients together with a whisk, a spoon, or a rotary or electric beater.

Blend means to stir rather than beat ingredients until they are thoroughly combined.

Bread Batter is a mixture of 1½ cups bread flour, 1 cup warm water and 1 tablespoon of active starter. It is aged for 24 hours at 75°. To work well, Bread Batter must be very active with the presence of wild yeast. Bread Batter or variations of it are the basis for all recipes in the bread section of this book.

Bread Flour is a somewhat gritty textured mixture of hard wheat flours. It is high in gluten (protein) and produces a very elastic dough which is a requirement of good bread.

Cake Flour is a very finely ground flour made from soft wheats. It greatly aids in producing fine, light, moist cakes. Cake flour is low in gluten.

Coat a Spoon is a term that describes the degree of thickness of a cooking liquid. To test for thickness, stir the liquid with a spoon. When the spoon is held above the pan and allowed to drip, it will retain an even film or coating of the liquid.

Cream means to soften solid fats such as butter, often by adding another ingredient such as sugar. Work the fat around the inside of a bowl by pressing and beating it with a spoon until it is soft and creamy.

Cut in is a method of combining solid fat with flour in biscuit making. Use your fingers, a pastry blender or two knives in a cutting motion to break the fat into small pieces. Mix throughout the flour. The resulting mixture should have a coarse, mealy consistency.

Deep Fry is to cook food immersed in hot fat or oil.

Dot means to place small pieces of butter or other fats over the surface of food.

Dough is a mixture of sourdough batter (Ambrosia or Bread), flour and additional ingredients. Dough is worked with the hands (kneaded) so that its ingredients are mixed and, in the case of bread, its gluten developed.

Fold means to incorporate an aerated mixture into a thicker, heavier one so that the character of the

126

lighter one is retained. To fold stiffly beaten egg whites into a batter, spoon a small portion of the egg whites onto the surface of the batter. With a rubber spatula cut down through the center of the whites to the bottom of the bowl or pan, slide the spatula along the bottom to the edge and bring it back up to the top. Gradually fold in the rest of the egg whites with vertical cutting strokes until all the whites have been absorbed. This should be a quick but gentle operation.

Fry is to cook in a small quantity of hot fat or oil. As opposed to deep frying, the oil in a pan or griddle comprises only a very thin coating.

Gluten is a baker's term for the protein which is present in a hard wheat flour. As the protein (gluten) in a dough made with bread flour is kneaded, it becomes very elastic. See page 99 for tests to check gluten development.

Knead (biscuit dough) is to manipulate the dough so that the ingredients are mixed. The dough is first shaped into a ball and then pushed down with the heel of the hand, then reshaped and pushed down again. This operation is repeated for 15 strokes, about 20 to 30 seconds.

Knead (bread dough) is to work the dough vigorously to mix the ingredients and develop the gluten. As with biscuit dough, bread dough is shaped into a ball and then pushed down with the heel of the hand. This is repeated until the dough starts to become elastic. At this point it is no longer necessary to reshape the dough with each knead. Roll the dough under the hand as if it were a rubber ball. Turn it occasionally for a new angle of attack. As dough is kneaded, the gluten is more thoroughly and completely developed when the fingers are dug into it. A finished dough with proper gluten development will require from 200 to 300 forceful strokes. This will take from 10 to 20 minutes. A dough with proper gluten development will be very stretchy and elastic.

127

Leaven means the same as to raise.

Melt is to change fat and solid dissolvable foods into a liquid state by heating.

Pastry flour is similar to cake flour but is not so finely ground. It is made from soft wheat and is excellent for biscuits. Pastry flour is low in gluten.

Preheat means to heat an oven to a desired temperature for about 15 minutes before using. Home kitchen ovens heat from both the top and the bottom when set on preheat. For this reason, the preheat setting is unsuitable for baking.

Rest (as with dough) refers to allowing a batter or bread dough to sit a few minutes before handling it again.

Raise refers to the action of wild yeast on a dough, causing it to puff up as a result of the release of CO_2.

Roux is a mixture of flour and fat, cooked and then used as a thickening agent for a sauce or gravy.

Scald means to heat a liquid to just below a boil. The scalding of fresh milk destroys the enzymes which interfere with the fermentation of wild yeast.

Separate (as with eggs) means to divide the yolk from the white of the egg. To separate egg yolks from the whites, separate the two halves of the shell, letting some of the white drip into a bowl. Slide the egg yolk into your hand, letting the rest of the white run between your fingers into a bowl, and place the yolk in a separate bowl. Or crack the egg in half and carefully pour the yolk back and forth from one half of the shell to the other, letting the white run into a bowl.

128 **Steam** means to cook by means of vapor from boiling water rising around the food.

To flour means to evenly cover with a thin layer of flour. To coat a baking pan with flour, first rub grease on the inner surfaces of the pan, then shake the flour and rotate the pan until a thin, even layer adheres to the sides and bottom. Turn the pan upside-down and rap it against a solid surface to dislodge excess flour.

Turn onto refers to taking a partially mixed dough from the bowl and placing on a bread board for kneading.

Whip means to beat quickly and steadily, either by hand with a whisk or rotary beater or with an electric beater. Whipping adds air to a liquid, such as heavy cream, and thereby increases its volume and lightens its consistency.

RECIPE INDEX

131